GUIDELINES FOR PREPARATION OF EARLY CHILDHOOD PROFESSIONALS

A 1995–96 NAEYC Comprehensive Membership benefit

National Association for the Education of Young Children
Washington, D.C.

Section 3—Reprinted by permission of the National Board for Professional Teaching Standards (NBPTS), © 1995, all rights reserved.

National Association for the Education
of Young Children
1509 16th Street, NW
Washington DC 20036-1426
202-232-8777 or 800-424-2460
Fax 202-328-1846

The National Association for the Education of Young Children (NAEYC) attempts through its publications program to provide a forum for discussion of major issues and ideas in our field. We hope to provoke thought and promote professional growth. The views expressed here are endorsed by all the participating associations. NAEYC wishes to thank the organizations contributing to this book.

Library of Congress Catalog Card Number: 96-69839
ISBN Catalog Number: 0-935989-77-3
NAEYC #212

Printed in the United States of America.

CONTENTS

SECTION 2. DEC/CEC PERSONNEL STANDARDS FOR EARLY EDUCATION AND EARLY INTERVENTION: GUIDELINES FOR LICENSURE IN EARLY CHILDHOOD SPECIAL EDUCATION

SECTION 3. NBPTS STANDARDS FOR EARLY CHILDHOOD/GENERALIST CERTIFICATION

PREFACE

A growing body of research supports the value of high-quality early childhood programs for children's later success in school and in life. Although early childhood programs have the potential for producing positive and lasting effects on children, this potential will not be achieved unless more attention is paid to ensuring that all programs meet the highest standards of quality, the most important determinant of which is the teacher. Early childhood education, like all education, demands well-prepared teachers.

The purpose of this book is to articulate the early childhood profession's agreed-upon standards for the preparation of early childhood professionals. Section 1 provides guidelines for program planners and evaluators by articulating the outcomes of early childhood preparation programs at the associate, baccalaureate, and advanced (master's and doctoral) levels. These guidelines were developed by NAEYC and endorsed by the Association of Teacher Educators (ATE) and the Division for Early Childhood of the Council for Exceptional Children (DEC/CEC). These guidelines are designed to help institutions develop programs and also to provide guidance to states in setting standards for licensure of teachers. In keeping with the trends toward performance-based licensure and accreditation, these guidelines are framed as candidate performances. NAEYC's guidelines for baccalaureate and advanced programs are also approved by the National Council for Accreditation of Teacher Education (NCATE) and are used by institutions seeking NCATE accreditation. Section 1 of this book includes directions for institutions that are preparing an NCATE Folio for which they are seeking NAEYC approval.

Section 2 addresses the professional preparation of early childhood special educators. The guidelines were developed by DEC and were endorsed by NAEYC and ATE. These guidelines describe the content of baccalaureate level preparation for early childhood special educators and offer recommendations for state licensure as well.

The guidelines in Sections 1 and 2 describe the outcomes of early childhood education and early childhood special education professional preparation programs and initial licensure of teachers. Section 3 provides a description of accomplished early childhood teaching as envisioned by the Early Childhood/Generalist Committee of the National Board for Professional Teaching Standards (NBPTS). The NBPTS certifies accomplished teachers, who must have at least a baccalaureate degree and three years of teaching to be eligible. The NBPTS standards for the early childhood certificate are generally congruent with NAEYC's guidelines for professional preparation and were endorsed by the NAEYC Governing Board; although NBPTS defines early childhood as ages 3 through 8, and NAEYC defines it as birth through age 8. Early childhood preparation programs at all levels can benefit from recognizing the long-term outcome goals envisioned in the NBPTS standards and go beyond them by preparing their graduates to work with infants and toddlers as well.

The diversity of the early childhood profession, with various settings and levels, has been characterized by NAEYC as a career lattice rather than a career ladder (Bredekamp & Willer 1992; Johnson & McCracken 1994). What unifies this diverse field as a profession is shared knowledge (Bredekamp 1996). The shared knowledge of early childhood education constitutes the content of the early childhood professional preparation curriculum, as described in the various sets of standards included in this book.

—Sue Bredekamp
NAEYC Director of
Professional Development

REFERENCES

Bredekamp, S. 1996. Early childhood education. In *Handbook of research on teacher education,* 2d ed., ed. J. Sikula, 323–47. New York: Macmillan.

Bredekamp, S., & B. Willer. 1992. Of ladders and lattices, cores and cones: Conceptualizing an early childhood professional development system. *Young Children* 47 (3): 47–50.

Johnson, J., & J.B. McCracken, eds. 1994. *The early childhood career lattice: Perspectives on professional development.* Washington, DC: NAEYC.

ACKNOWLEDGMENT

NAEYC wishes to thank its Professional Development Panel—individuals who have previously served and those who continue in three-year terms of service. This body of nationally known experts in content, delivery system issues, and policy have assisted in developing and reviewing various sets of standards and procedures for the review of professional development programs. Their recommendations to the NAEYC Governing Board and staff have helped toward achieving NAEYC's goal of an articulated system of early childhood professional preparation and development.

SECTION 1. NAEYC GUIDELINES FOR PREPARATION OF EARLY CHILDHOOD PROFESSIONALS

INTRODUCTION

NAEYC guidelines describe the common core of knowledge, performances, and dispositions that are desired outcomes of preparation programs for early childhood professionals. Early childhood education is a diverse field and it encompasses many roles in addition to the traditional role of "teacher." NAEYC defines *early childhood settings* as including but not limited to any part- or full-day program in a center, school, or home that serves children from birth through age 8 and their families, including children with special developmental and learning needs. This definition includes programs in child care centers, both for-profit and nonprofit; private and public prekindergarten programs; Head Start programs; family child care; and kindergartens, primary grades, and before- and after-school programs in elementary schools (NAEYC 1994).

This diverse field is unified by a common core of knowledge that deepens and expands with specializations at higher levels of preparation. At the associate level, the graduate demonstrates knowledge of theory and practices necessary to plan and implement curriculum for individual children and groups; in addition, at the baccalaureate level, the graduate demonstrates the ability to apply and analyze the core knowledge and to systematically develop curriculum, and develop and conduct assessments of individual children and groups. At the master's level, the graduate demonstrates greater capacity to analyze and refine the core knowledge and evaluate and apply research to improve practices; at the doctoral level, the graduate conducts research and studies practices to expand the knowledge base

and influence systems change. At each of these levels, the professional is expected to reflect on his or her practices that result in improved programming for children and also contribute to continuing professional development. In addition, at each of these levels, the professional is expected to advocate for policies designed to improve conditions for children, families, and the profession.

The guidelines also reflect the recent shift toward providing services for children with disabilities in inclusive settings. Federal laws, the Individuals with Disabilities Education Act (IDEA) and the Americans with Disabilities Act (ADA), ensure that all early childhood programs must be prepared to serve children with disabilities and developmental delays as well as children at risk for developmental delays. Such inclusive practice necessitates inclusive philosophy and inclusive professional preparation.

The guidelines are framed as outcomes rather than processes, in keeping with performance-based teacher education standards promoted by the National Council for the Accreditation of Teacher Education (NCATE 1995) and performance-based licensure systems emerging in states throughout the nation. In addition, focusing on the outcomes of preparation recognizes the need for and value of various routes to achieving these outcomes. This document does not promote any single route to the acquisition of an early childhood certificate, license, or degree but rather calls for all teachers of young children from birth through age 8 to be adequately prepared to demonstrate the knowledge, performance, and disposition specific to their teaching specialization, regardless of their employment setting or their position.

To achieve the goal of qualified early childhood professionals working with all children, it is recommended (ATE & NAEYC 1991) that state departments of education and other bodies responsible for enforcing standards of personnel qualifications address the following policies:

- The unique learning needs of children, birth through age 8, are acknowledged as a distinctive knowledge base requiring a freestanding licensure (certification) distinctive from existing elementary and secondary licenses (certifications).
- The degree, licensure, or certification standards are age and content congruent across the 50 states to have truly reciprocal agreements and to ensure that all children are cared for and educated by teachers appropriately prepared as early childhood educators.
- All teacher preparation programs meet the minimum standards set forth in this document.
- All early childhood teacher preparation programs, especially in the configuration and coordination of their individual programs, recognize the inseparability of the care *and* the education of young children.
- States initiate articulation agreements between two-year and four-year institutions within a state to provide a continuum of teacher preparation opportunities that reflect total educational background and competencies, promote professional development, and ensure access to the profession.
- States create ways to coordinate the efforts of those departments that credential professionals in child care settings and in public and private schools.

The format and content of these guidelines are based on the position statement "Early Childhood Teacher Certification" developed by ATE and NAEYC (1991), "Early Childhood Baccalaureate Teacher Certification Standards" (NAECS/SDE and NAECTE 1993), draft "Model Standards for Beginning Teacher Licensing and Development" developed by the Interstate New Teacher Assessment and Support Consortium (CCSSO 1992), the personnel preparation recommendations of DEC (1993; ATE, DEC, & NAEYC 1994), and the earlier versions of the associate, basic, and advanced guidelines (NAEYC 1985, 1991).

REFERENCES

Association of Teacher Educators (ATE), & National Association for the Education of Young Children (NAEYC). 1991. Early childhood teacher certification. *Young Children* 47 (1): 16–21.

Association of Teacher Educators (ATE), Division for Early Childhood (DEC), & National Association for the Education of Young Children (NAEYC). 1994. Personnel standards for early education and early intervention: A position of ATE, DEC, and NAEYC. In *NAEYC position statements,* 127–29. Washington, DC: NAEYC.

Council of Chief State School Officers (CCSSO)/Interstate New Teacher Assessment and Support Consortium. 1992. Model standards for beginning teacher licensing and development: A resource for state dialogue. Working paper. Washington, DC: Author.

Division for Early Childhood (DEC)/Council for Exceptional Children. 1993. *DEC-recommended practices: Indicators of quality in programs for infants and young children with special needs and their families.* Reston, VA: Council for Exceptional Children.

National Association for the Education of Young Children (NAEYC). 1994. NAEYC position statement: A conceptual framework for early childhood professional development. *Young Children* 49 (3): 68–77.

National Association of Early Childhood Specialists in State Departments of Education (NAECS/SDE), & National Association of Early Childhood Teacher Educators (NAECTE). 1993. Early childhood baccalaureate teacher certification standards. *Journal of Early Childhood Teacher Education* (winter): 13–16.

National Council for Accreditation of Teacher Education. 1995. *Standards, procedures, and policies for the accreditation of professional education units.* Washington, DC: Author.

GUIDELINES FOR EARLY CHILDHOOD PROFESSIONAL PREPARATION PROGRAMS AT THE ASSOCIATE, BACCALAUREATE, AND ADVANCED LEVELS

I.
Design of Professional Education

The overall design of the early childhood professional preparation program derives from and is consistent with a coherent conceptual framework that reflects current interdisciplinary knowledge about the preparation of early childhood professionals. The design of professional education creates an environment conducive to continuous learning and professional growth for all participants.

A. CONCEPTUAL FRAMEWORK

1. The professional preparation program is derived from a conceptual framework that is knowledge based; shared among faculty, candidates, and other community members; and written, well articulated, and regularly evaluated.

2. Coherence exists among the conceptual framework and the student outcomes, courses, field experiences, teaching and learning practices, and evaluation.

3. The program ensures that candidates can integrate general knowledge, content knowledge, and professional and pedagogical knowledge to create meaningful learning experiences for all children and to support families.

4. The program ensures that candidates develop awareness and sensitivity to issues of diversity and discrimination and are prepared to work in programs serving diverse populations of children and their families, including children with disabilities.

5. The program prepares candidates to work in collaboration with families, policymakers, community agencies, and professionals from their own and other disciplines.

B. GENERAL STUDIES

The program of general studies ensures that candidates are broadly educated individuals who can communicate effectively and who understand the key concepts and tools of inquiry of the various disciplines that form and influence the basis for the early childhood curriculum.

1. The program ensures that candidates develop theoretical and practical knowledge in humanities, mathematics and technology, social sciences, biological and physical sciences, the arts, and personal health and fitness.

2. General studies incorporates multicultural and global perspectives.

C. CONTENT STUDIES

The program ensures that candidates attain competence in early childhood education as described in the guidelines for the associate and the baccalaureate levels (page 13) or the advanced level (page 21).

D. QUALITY OF TEACHING AND LEARNING

1. The program requires that candidates integrate theories of child development, family systems, theories of learning, content knowledge, and early childhood curriculum and pedagogy with application during field experiences.

2. Teaching in the program is consistent with the conceptual framework, reflects knowledge derived from research and content disciplines and sound professional practice, and is of high quality.

3. Teaching and learning reflects knowledge about and experiences with diverse populations and is based on knowledge of cultural and individual adult learning styles.

4. Program faculty use a variety of methods and strategies, such as case method, inquiry-centered problem solving, collaborative group work, interactive strategies, reflective writing and discussion, direct instruction, role playing, and appropriate use of technology to support teaching and learning.

5. The learning environment encourages and supports the candidate to be reflective and actively engaged in the learning process.

6. Teaching and learning are continuously evaluated, and results are used to improve the program and to assure that candidates achieve and are able to implement the curriculum outcomes.

7. Physical environments and teaching and learning are adapted to meet the special needs of candidates.

E. QUALITY OF FIELD EXPERIENCES

Candidates have the opportunity to participate in high-quality field experiences. The need for and types of supervised field experiences are based on candidate's prior training or experiences, and faculty will ensure that candidates have had supervised field experiences at the associate or baccalaureate level. Advanced level candidates are expected to have previously completed field experiences; if not, the following guidelines apply.

1. Standards are established and used by the program for selection and evaluation of appropriate field sites and cooperating personnel.

2. Field experiences are consistent with the conceptual framework, are well planned and sequenced, are of high quality, and provide ample opportunity for candidates to integrate theory and practice.

3. Experience with children and families in field settings is an early and continuing part of the program. Such experience is supervised and evaluated by qualified faculty and may include child-study observations, field-based methods courses, development and implementation of learning experiences for children, tutoring, and student teaching. Experience with families may include home visits, parent-teacher conferences, small-group meetings for parents, reporting to parents, and consultations regarding referrals.

4. Field experiences provide candidates with opportunities to study and practice in a variety of settings, with children of different ages and their families, in diverse types of settings, with children and families who are culturally and linguistically diverse, and with children with disabilities or special learning and developmental needs.

5. Field experience provides candidates with opportunities to learn how to work in collaboration with field-site staff, to work as a member of an interdisciplinary team, and to reflect on their practice in collaborative relationships.

6. Field-experience placements reflect the best possible current practices in early childhood education. The NAEYC and the DEC/CEC (Division of Early Childhood/Council for Exceptional Children) criteria for high-quality programs are used to evaluate field placements.

II.
Candidates in Professional Education

Candidates in the program demonstrate the knowledge and abilities necessary to perform successfully as early childhood professionals.

A. QUALIFICATIONS

1. The program recruits and admits candidates who demonstrate potential for success in the early childhood profession as defined by faculty at the institution.

2. The program endeavors to retain and graduate those who demonstrate success in the early childhood program.

B. COMPOSITION

1. The institution has and implements an explicit plan with adequate resources to recruit, admit, support, and retain a diverse student body.

2. The program recruits, admits, supports, and retains a diverse student body.

C. MONITORING AND ADVISING THE PROGRESS OF CANDIDATES

1. Candidates' progress is assessed in multiple ways based on multiple sources of information and authentic, performance-based assessment methods.

2. The program ensures that candidates have access to a comprehensive advisement system, including appropriate academic and professional advisement from admission through completion of their professional education.

3. The program faculty review the performance of candidates on a regular basis and provide advice and counseling regarding their continuation in the program and the profession.

4. The program provides candidates opportunities for scholarly interaction beyond course requirements and for the development of mentor/protégé relationships.

D. ENSURING THE COMPETENCE OF CANDIDATES

1. The program provides candidates with multiple opportunities for reflection and self-assessment.

2. The program ensures that candidates demonstrate verbal and written abilities to communicate effectively with children, families, and other professionals.

3. The program ensures that a candidate's competency to begin his or her professional role as described in the curriculum outcomes (pp. 13–24) is assessed at regular intervals prior to completion of the program.

4. Faculty inform candidates in writing of the various criteria upon which their progress is assessed and their competencies are evaluated.

5. Faculty assess candidates' mastery of the program's stated exit criteria or outcomes through the use of multiple sources of data, such as a culminating experience, portfolios, interviews with faculty and parents, videotaped and observed performance in early childhood programs, standardized tests, scholarly papers, dissertations, theses, and course grades or written evaluations for institutions that do not give grades.

6. The program ensures that candidates abide by professional ethics and that they demonstrate competencies with children, families, and other adults.

7. Advanced programs for the continuing preparation of teachers or other school personnel build upon and extend prior knowledge and experiences that include core understanding of learning and practices that support learning.

8. Candidates in advanced programs enhance their ability to use research, research methods, and knowledge about issues and trends to improve practice with children and families.

III.
Professional Education Faculty

The professional relationships within the early childhood professional preparation program provide an appropriate model of ethical, professional, and collaborative behavior for candidates in their interactions with children, families, colleagues, and other professionals. Standards should apply to all faculty, whether hired on a temporary, part-time, or full-time basis.

A. QUALIFICATIONS

1. All faculty are academically qualified for their specific professional roles, have had direct, substantial, successful professional experience, and continue to enhance their expertise in the early childhood profession.

2. Faculty have completed formal advanced study and have demonstrated competence through scholarly activities in each field of specialization that they teach.

3. Faculty model actions consistent with the Code of Ethical Conduct (Feeney & Kipnis [1989] 1992) in dealing with administrators, colleagues, students, families, and children.

B. COMPOSITION

1. The program recruits, hires, mentors, and retains a diverse faculty.

2. The institution has and implements an explicit recruiting policy with adequate resources to ensure hiring and retaining a diverse faculty.

3. The institution's efforts and success in meeting goals for recruiting a diverse faculty are evaluated annually, and appropriate steps are taken to strengthen plans for the future, based on the annual evaluation.

C. PROFESSIONAL ASSIGNMENTS OF FACULTY

1. Work assignments accommodate faculty involvement in teaching, scholarship, and service, including curriculum development and evaluation, advising and mentoring, collaboration with families and other professionals, scholarly activities, and service to the institution, profession, and community.

2. Faculty teaching responsibilities, including overloads and off-campus teaching, are mutually agreed upon and designed to allow faculty to engage effectively in teaching, scholarship, service, and interdisciplinary collaboration.

D. PROFESSIONAL DEVELOPMENT OF FACULTY

1. Faculty members maintain currency in the field through active participation in appropriate professional organizations, conferences, scholarly study, and service to the profession.

2. Faculty members have opportunities to develop knowledge and collaborative relationships with professionals in other disciplines.

3. Faculty members' performance is periodically reviewed and evaluated; the review includes self-assessment and reflection, professional early childhood peer evaluations, and assessment by other individuals.

4. The program provides opportunities for faculty development, such as travel support, leave, inservice training, education visits, exchanges, and fellowships.

Feeney, S., & K. Kipnis. [1989] 1992. *Code of ethical conduct & statement of commitment.* Washington, DC: NAEYC.

IV.
Administration of the Early Childhood Professional Preparation Program

The interdisciplinary focus of early childhood professional preparation programs as well as the field's diverse history and service delivery systems require a collaborative approach to professional preparation. Because the education of early childhood professionals occurs in a variety of schools, departments, and colleges at many institutions, it is essential that the administrative structure facilitates rather than impedes candidates' progress through the program.

A. GOVERNANCE AND ACCOUNTABILITY

1. The program is organized, coordinated, and unified to ensure the fulfillment of the program's mission and to facilitate candidates' progress through the program.

2. The program is articulated with related institutions, programs, and other disciplines serving young children and their families, or program faculty are working toward articulation through participation on state committees or similar activities.

3. Programs are responsive to local and state educational needs, participating in partnerships, as appropriate, within the local community and the state.

4. Faculty participate in programmatic decisions and are represented on higher-level decisionmaking bodies of the institution.

5. Faculty regularly engage in program evaluation and development.

6. Programs are revised appropriately, based on the results of regular evaluation and needs assessments and on new knowledge about the education of children, relationships with families, and the education of professionals.

7. Candidates participate in evaluation of courses, faculty, field experiences, and the program.

B. RESOURCES

1. Adequate funding is provided to ensure high-quality early childhood professional preparation, including a reasonable ratio of candidates to faculty to promote learning, opportunity for faculty collaboration, support for faculty to engage in professional development, extensive supervised field experiences, and a wide array of current professional materials.

2. Faculty have access to and use of state-of-the-art instructional materials and technology, including early childhood classroom materials, consumable supplies, video and other media equipment, and computers.

3. Access to a comprehensive support system (e.g., academic, financial, personal) is available to ensure that candidates have every opportunity to succeed in the program.

4. Facilities and equipment are safe, attractive, functional, and well maintained.

5. Teaching and learning occur in spaces and environmental arrangements that promote student involvement and allow for a variety of methods that model practices for candidates to implement with children.

6. The institution's library reflects a commitment to child development and early childhood education. A sufficient number of current books, journals, periodicals, media, and other materials that reflect the diversity of philosophy in the field are available. Adequate library resources include but are not limited to study space for students; instructional and

curriculum laboratories; state-of-the-art media and data-processing and technological equipment; and cooperative educational and research relationships with early childhood settings and practitioners.

7. Candidates have access to resources and strategies to effectively collaborate with and support families, interdisciplinary professionals, and personnel in community agencies.

8. Career counseling and placement resources are available to candidates. Candidates receive adequate individual assessment and professional advisement.

9. Budget trends over the past five years and future planning indicate adequate support for the early childhood professional preparation programs that allow them to meet expected outcomes.

10. Faculty have access to support staff, such as secretaries and assistants.

11. Placement services for qualified graduates are developed and maintained, giving a widespread opportunity to graduates.

ASSOCIATE AND BACCALAUREATE DEGREES

Introduction

The development of knowledgeable and competent professionals to work with young children and their families is a continuous process. The graduate of an early childhood preparation program has acquired a core of knowledge that includes the foundation for a philosophy of teaching and learning; a broad base of knowledge of child development, both typical and atypical, from birth through age 8 from which their work with young children emerges; and special competence in working with children, both with and without disabilities, in at least two periods of the broader age span (infant/toddler, preprimary, or primary-school age). Competence in working with all young children from birth through age 8 is attained through further study and experience.

These guidelines describe the common core of professional knowledge and abilities needed by all early childhood educators. Much of this core is similar at the associate and baccalaureate levels; to some extent the core of knowledge and skills is a recursive cycle with content revisited in greater depth and breadth at higher levels. Another differentiation between baccalaureate and associate programs is the continuum of general knowledge that is increased in a four- or five-year program. Broad general knowledge constitutes the "content" of the curriculum for children. Children want and need to learn about everything—science, social studies, literature, math, music, and everything else in their world of experience. To provide experiences that reflect this broad content requires knowledgeable professionals. A crucial interaction takes place between professional knowledge and general knowledge; at higher levels of preparation, professional knowledge is embedded within a broader context of greater breadth and depth of knowledge that is important for increasing understanding and for generating new knowledge.

Preparation standards are necessary for individuals functioning in a variety of roles. These guidelines address the preparation of early childhood educators who work directly with young children in a variety of early childhood settings, who must accommodate children with a range of abilities and special needs and who must work collaboratively with families and other professionals (ATE, DEC, & NAEYC 1994; see reference on p. 4). Standards for preparation of early childhood special educators and related services personnel are addressed in Section 2.

The qualified early childhood educator will demonstrate professional knowledge, abilities, dispositions, values, and attitudes regarding child development and learning, curriculum development and implementation, family and community relationships, assessment and evaluation, professionalism, and practice during field experiences.

Guidelines for Associate Degree-Granting Institutions and Technical Schools

1. Child Development and Learning. Programs prepare early childhood professionals who

    1.1 Use knowledge of how children develop and learn to provide opportunities that support the physical, social, emotional, language, cognitive, and aesthetic development of all young children from birth through age 8.

    1.2 Use knowledge of how young children differ in their development and approaches to learning to support the development and learning of individual children.

    1.3 Create and modify environments and experiences to meet the individual needs of all children, including children with disabilities, developmental delays, and special abilities.

    1.4 Apply knowledge of cultural and linguistic diversity to create environments and experiences that affirm and respect culturally and linguistically diverse children, support home-language preservation, and promote antibias approaches and the valuing of diversity.

2. Curriculum Development and Implementation. Programs prepare early childhood professionals who

    2.1 Plan and implement developmentally appropriate curriculum and instructional practices based on knowledge of individual children, the community, and curriculum goals and content through the following actions:

        2.1.1 use developmentally appropriate methods that include play, small-group projects, open-ended questioning, group discussion, problem solving, cooperative learning, and inquiry experiences to help young children develop intellectual curiosity, solve problems, make decisions, and become critical thinkers;

        2.1.2 use a variety of strategies to encourage children's physical, social, emotional, aesthetic, and cognitive development;

        2.1.3 demonstrate current knowledge of and ability to implement meaningful, integrated learning experiences in curriculum content areas, including language and literacy, mathematics, science, health, safety, nutrition, social studies, the arts, music, drama, and movement;

        2.1.4 plan and implement an integrated curriculum that focuses on children's needs and interests and takes into account culturally valued content and children's home experiences;

        2.1.5 create, evaluate, and select developmentally appropriate materials, equipment, and environments; and

        2.1.6 adapt strategies and environments to meet the specific needs of children with disabilities, developmental delays, or special abilities.

2.2 Use individual and group guidance and problem-solving techniques to develop positive and supportive relationships with children, encourage positive social interaction among children, promote positive strategies of conflict resolution, and to develop personal self-control, self-motivation, and self-esteem in children.

2.3 Integrate goals from IEPs (Individual Education Plan) and IFSPs (Individual Family Service Plan) into daily activities and routines.

2.4 Establish and maintain physically and psychologically safe and healthy learning environments for children through the following actions:

2.4.1 demonstrate understanding of the developmental consequences of stress and trauma; protective factors, resilience, and the development of mental health; and the importance of supportive relationships with adults and peers;

2.4.2 implement basic health, nutrition, and safety management practices for young children, including specific procedures for infants and toddlers and procedures regarding childhood illness and communicable diseases;

2.4.3 use appropriate health-appraisal procedures and recommend referral to appropriate community health and social services when necessary; and

2.4.4 recognize signs of emotional distress, child abuse, and neglect in young children and know responsibility and procedures for reporting known or suspected abuse or neglect to appropriate authorities.

3. Family and Community Relationships. Programs prepare early childhood professionals who

3.1 Establish and maintain positive, collaborative relationships with families by the following means:

3.1.1 respect parents' choices and goals for children and communicate effectively with parents about curriculum and children's progress; and

3.1.2 involve families in planning for individual children, including children with disabilities, developmental delays, or special abilities.

3.2 Demonstrate sensitivity to differences in family structures and social and cultural backgrounds.

3.3 Communicate effectively with other professionals concerned with children and with agencies in the larger community to support children's development, learning, and well-being.

4. Assessment. Programs prepare early childhood professionals who

4.1 Use informal assessment strategies to plan and individualize curriculum and teaching practices to meet the needs of individual children and to ensure the continuous physical, social, emotional, aesthetic, and cognitive development of children.

4.2 Observe, record, and assess young children's development and learning for the purpose of planning appropriate programs, environments, and interactions, and adapting for individual differences, including children with special needs.

5. Professionalism. Programs prepare early childhood professionals who

5.1 Reflect on their practices, articulate a philosophy and rationale for decisions, and continually self-assess and evaluate the effects of their choices and actions on others (young children, parents, and other professionals) as a basis for program planning and modification and continuing professional development.

5.2 Demonstrate an understanding of conditions of children, families, and professionals; current issues and trends; legal issues; and legislation and other public policies affecting children, families, and programs for young children and the early childhood profession.

5.3 Demonstrate an understanding of the early childhood profession, its historical, philosophical, and social foundations and how these foundations influence current thought and practice.

5.4 Demonstrate awareness of and commitment to the profession's Code of Ethical Conduct.

5.5 Actively seek out opportunities to grow professionally by locating and using appropriate professional literature, organizations, resources, and experiences to inform and improve practice.

5.6 Establish and maintain positive, collaborative relationships with colleagues, other professionals, and families, and work effectively as a member of a professional team.

5.7 Serve as advocates on behalf of young children and their families, improved quality of programs and services for young children, and enhanced professional status and working conditions for early childhood educators.

6. Field Experiences. Programs prepare early childhood professionals who

6.1. Observe and participate under supervision of qualified professionals in a variety of settings in which young children from birth through age 8 are served, and work effectively over time with children of diverse ages (infants, toddlers, preschoolers, or primary-school age), children with diverse abilities, and children reflecting culturally and linguistically diverse family systems and in diverse settings (such as public and private; centers, schools, and community agencies).

6.2. Work effectively over time with children of diverse ages (infants, toddlers, preschoolers, or primary-school age), children with diverse abilities, and children reflecting culturally and linguistically diverse family systems.

6.3 Demonstrate ability to work effectively during at least 300 clock hours of supervised student teaching and/or practica experiences in appropriate settings serving infants, toddlers, preschoolers, or children of primary-school age.

Guidelines for Four- and Five-Year Institutions (Initial Certification)

1. Child Development and Learning. Programs prepare early childhood professionals who

1.1 Use knowledge of how children develop and learn to provide opportunities that support the physical, social, emotional, language, cognitive, and aesthetic development of all young children from birth through age 8.

1.2 Use knowledge of how young children differ in their development and approaches to learning to support the development and learning of individual children in the following ways:

1.2.1 demonstrate understanding of the conditions that affect children's development and learning, including risk factors, developmental variations, and developmental patterns of specific disabilities; and

1.2.2 create and modify environments and experiences to meet the individual needs of all children, including children with disabilities, developmental delays, and special abilities.

1.3 Apply knowledge of cultural and linguistic diversity and the significance of sociocultural and political contexts for development and learning; recognize that children are best understood in the contexts of family, culture, and society; and thus

1.3.1 demonstrate understanding of the interrelationships among culture, language, and thought and of the function of the home language in the development of young children; and

1.3.2 affirm and respect culturally and linguistically diverse children, support home-language preservation, and promote antibias approaches

through the creation of learning environments and experiences.

2. Curriculum Development and Implementation. Programs prepare early childhood professionals who

2.1 Plan and implement developmentally appropriate curriculum and instructional practices, based on knowledge of individual children, the community, and curriculum goals and content, in the following ways:

2.1.1 use and explain the rationale for developmentally appropriate methods that include play, small-group projects, open-ended questioning, group discussion, problem solving, cooperative learning, and inquiry experiences to help young children develop intellectual curiosity, solve problems, and make decisions;

2.1.2 use a variety of strategies to encourage children's physical, social, emotional, aesthetic, and cognitive development;

2.1.3 demonstrate current knowledge of and ability to develop and implement meaningful, integrated learning experiences, using the central concepts and tools of inquiry in curriculum content areas, including language and literacy, mathematics, science, health, safety, nutrition, social studies, art, music, drama, and movement;

2.1.4 develop and implement an integrated curriculum that focuses on children's needs and interests and takes into account culturally valued content and children's home experiences;

2.1.5 create, evaluate, and select appropriate developmentally appropriate materials, equipment, and environments;

2.1.6 evaluate and demonstrate appropriate use of technology with young children, including assistive technologies for children with disabilities;

2.1.7 develop and evaluate topics of study in terms of conceptual soundness, significance, and intellectual integrity; and

2.1.8 adapt strategies and environments to meet the specific needs of all children, including those with disabilities, developmental delays, or special abilities.

2.2 Use individual and group guidance and problem-solving techniques to develop positive and supportive relationships with children, encourage positive social interaction among children, promote positive strategies of conflict resolution, and develop personal self-control, self-motivation, and self-esteem.

2.3 Incorporate knowledge and strategies from multiple disciplines (for example, health and social services) into the design of intervention strategies and integrate goals from IEPs (Individual Education Plan) and IFSPs (Individual Family Service Plan) into daily activities and routines.

2.4 Establish and maintain physically and psychologically safe and healthy learning environments for children in the following ways:

2.4.1 demonstrate understanding of the influence of the physical setting, schedule, routines, and transitions on children and use these experiences to promote children's development and learning;

2.4.2 demonstrate understanding of the developmental consequences of stress and trauma, protective factors and resilience, the development of mental health, and the importance of supportive relationships;

2.4.3 implement basic health, nutrition, and safety management practices for young children, including specific procedures for infants and toddlers and procedures regarding childhood illness and communicable diseases;

2.4.4 use appropriate health-appraisal procedures and recommend referral to appropriate community health and social services when necessary; and

2.4.5 recognize signs of emotional distress, child abuse, and neglect in young children and know one's responsibility and the procedures for reporting known or suspected abuse or neglect to appropriate authorities.

3. Family and Community Relationships. Programs prepare early childhood professionals who

3.1 Establish and maintain positive, collaborative relationships with families by the following means:

3.1.1 respect parents' choices and goals for children and communicate effectively with parents about curriculum and children's progress;

3.1.2 involve families in assessing and planning for individual children, including children with disabilities, developmental delays, or special abilities; and

3.1.3 support parents in making decisions related to their child's development and their parenting.

3.2 Demonstrate sensitivity to differences in family structures and social and cultural backgrounds.

3.3 Apply family-systems theory and knowledge of the dynamics, roles, and relationships within families and communities.

3.4 Link families with a range of family-oriented services based on identified resources, priorities, and concerns.

3.5 Communicate effectively with other professionals concerned with children and with agencies in the larger community to support children's development, learning, and well-being.

4. Assessment and Evaluation.

4.1 Use informal and formal assessment strategies to plan and individualize curriculum and teaching practices through the following actions:

4.1.1 observe, record, and assess young children's development and learning and engage children in self-assessment for the purpose of planning appropriate programs, environments, and interactions and adapting for individual differences;

4.1.2 develop and use authentic, performance-based assessments of children's learning to assist in planning and to communicate with children and parents;

4.1.3 participate with and assist other professionals in conducting family-centered assessments;

4.1.4 select, evaluate, and interpret formal, standardized assessment instruments and information used in the assessment of children, and integrate authentic classroom assessment data with formal assessment information; and

4.1.5 communicate assessment results and integrate assessment results from others as an active participant in the development and implementa-

tion of IEP and IFSP goals for children with special developmental and learning needs.

4.2 Develop and use formative and summative program evaluation to ensure comprehensive quality of the total environment for children, families, and the community.

5. Professionalism. Programs prepare early childhood professionals who

5.1 Reflect on their practices, articulate a philosophy and rationale for decisions, and continually self-assess and evaluate the effects of their choices and actions on others (young children, parents, and other professionals) as a basis for program planning and modification and continuing professional development.

5.2 Demonstrate an understanding of conditions of children, families, and professionals; current issues and trends; legal issues; and legislation and other public policies affecting children, families, and programs for young children and the early childhood profession.

5.3 Demonstrate an understanding of the early childhood profession, its multiple historical, philosophical, and social foundations and how these foundations influence current thought and practice.

5.4 Demonstrate awareness of and commitment to the profession's Code of Ethical Conduct.

5.5 Actively seek out opportunities to grow professionally by locating and using appropriate professional literature, organizations, resources, and experiences to inform and improve practice.

5.6 Establish and maintain positive, collaborative relationships with colleagues, other professionals, and families and work effectively as a member of a professional team.

5.7 Serve as advocates on behalf of young children and their families, improved quality of programs and services for young children, and enhanced professional status and working conditions for early childhood educators.

5.8 Demonstrate an understanding of basic principles of administration, organization, and operation of early childhood programs, including supervision of staff and volunteers and program evaluation.

6. Field Experiences. Programs prepare early childhood professionals who

6.1 Observe and participate under supervision of qualified professionals in a variety of settings in which young children from birth through age 8 are served (such as both public and private; centers, schools, and community agencies).

6.2 Work effectively over time with children of diverse ages (infants, toddlers, preschoolers, or primary-school age), children with diverse abilities, and children reflecting culturally and linguistically diverse family systems.

6.3 Demonstrate ability to work effectively during full-time (totaling at least 300 clock hours) supervised student teaching and/or practica experiences in at least two different settings, serving children of two different age groups (infant/toddler, preprimary, or primary-school age) and with varying abilities.

6.4 Analyze and evaluate field experiences, including supervised experience in working with parents and supervised experience in working with interdisciplinary teams of professionals.

ADVANCED DEGREES

Introduction: Core Principles

Programs in early childhood education offering advanced degrees are administered within various institutional configurations. For example, they may be offered within specialized departments designated as early childhood education or as specializations within departments, such as curriculum and instruction, teaching and curriculum, special education, child and family studies, or human development.

Candidates for advanced degrees in early childhood education should have completed basic level study and practice (as described in the baccalaureate guidelines preceding) or should incorporate the essential components of such study into their graduate curriculum. Fifth-year initial certification programs, even those that result in master's degrees, are considered basic and must meet the baccalaureate guidelines (pp. 17–20) according to NCATE. Thus, the desired outcomes of an advanced degree program are in addition to those established for baccalaureate programs.

There are many kinds of advanced degree programs in early childhood education. All of these have comparable goals but differ primarily in the opportunities for depth and breadth of study and the nature of the career focus. The goals of master's and specialist's programs differ somewhat from those of doctoral programs. The focus of the master's/specialist's program is on the practice or the study of the practice of early childhood education. Typically, advanced degrees at the master's and specialist's levels prepare stu-dents for various professional roles in early childhood education. The master's/specialist's candidate either seeks to enhance competence within an existing career or to prepare for a position requiring levels of understanding and performance different from those the candidate already possesses. For example, a master's/specialist's candidate may engage in applied research, practice in teacher education and staff development, work with families, issues analysis and advocacy related to early childhood education, and/or program administration. The outcome for a master's candidate is improved professional development for a specific career role as well as preparation for ongoing study. The master's program should not serve only as the first level of doctoral work.

By contrast, the focus of the doctoral program is on the study of early childhood education and its practice, including aspects of child development, pedagogy, curriculum, policy analysis, history and philosophy, and basic and applied research. The primary outcome for the doctoral candidate is to become a leader for the field who influences the practice of early childhood education through the generation of knowledge; the education of early childhood professionals; the conduct of research on young children's development and learning; the development, implementation, and evaluation of curriculum; the administration of early childhood programs and services at the local, state, and national levels; and the analysis and generation of public policy related to early childhood education. Doctoral candidates demonstrate specialized knowledge and capability in at least one of these areas as well as the ability to generalize across the knowledge base and to anticipate future roles emerging as the field develops and expands. Specializations at the master's and/or doctoral levels, such as early childhood special education/early intervention, family support, administration, or other areas, require further specialized study and practice.

Guidelines for all Advanced Degree Candidates

MASTER'S AND DOCTORAL CANDIDATES

1. Extend their knowledge and understanding of the dominant theories of human and sociocultural development and learning through the life span; a knowledge of research on social, emotional, cognitive, language, aesthetic, motor, and perceptual development and learning in children from birth through age 8, including children with special developmental and learning needs and their families; and the understanding of the child in the family and cultural context.

2. Extend and further develop their knowledge and understanding of theories and content of curriculum and instruction and alternative models and methodologies.

3. Critically examine alternative perspectives regarding central issues in the field (for example, child development, programs for young children and their families, research priorities, or implications of issues for teacher education and staff development).

4. Extend their knowledge and ability to develop and use a variety of procedures for assessment of child development and learning, child care and early education environments, and early childhood education curricula; and the understanding of types, purposes, and appropriateness of various assessment procedures and instruments.

5. Develop and evaluate programs for children from a variety of diverse cultural and language backgrounds, as well as for children of different age and developmental levels, including children with disabilities, children with developmental delays, children who are at risk for developmental delays, and children with special abilities.

6. Apply interdisciplinary knowledge from such fields as sociology, psychology, health services, special education, history, philosophy, and anthropology to their practice in early childhood education.

7. Engage in reflective inquiry and demonstrate professional self-knowledge, for example, by collecting data about one's own practice and articulating a personal code of professional ethics.

8. Demonstrate the ability to work collaboratively as a team member with colleagues and other professionals to achieve goals for children and families.

9. Develop knowledge and skills required to serve as a mentor to others and a model of professional behavior for volunteers and other staff members.

MASTER'S/SPECIALIST'S CANDIDATES

10. Understand the sociocultural, historical, and political forces that influence the diverse delivery systems through which programs are offered for young children and their families (for example, social service agencies, public schools, and private enterprise).

11. Collect and interpret research, translate research findings into practice, demonstrate personal research skills, and implement applied research.

12. Demonstrate deeper understanding of a particular area of specialization related to an intended career role (for example, administration and supervision of early childhood programs, family support programs, primary-grade teaching or administration, early childhood special education/early intervention, or infant/toddler programming).

13. Apply theoretical and research knowledge to practice in early childhood settings (their own classroom or other field assignments). For example, applications of theory to practice may be demonstrated during field study projects, action research, curriculum projects, or clinical practice observation.

14. Perform as reflective professionals capable of taking leadership roles in schools or programs, mentoring novice teachers, and acting as advocates for children at local, state, and national levels.

DOCTORAL CANDIDATES

15. Understand the diversity of delivery systems through which programs are offered for young children and their families (for example, social service agencies, public schools, or private enterprise) and become advocates for providing families with coordinated, quality services that are accessible and affordable. Doctoral candidates demonstrate understanding of the implications of contrasting missions, mores, resources, constraints, and potential of each system for preparing personnel to work in those settings.

16. Understand research methods and findings, are able to translate research findings into practice, demonstrate personal research skills and the ability to develop and implement applied research, and show the disposition to create and disseminate new knowledge.

17. Demonstrate deeper understanding of and exemplary practice in at least one area of specialization (for example, teacher education, assessment and evaluation, early childhood special education/early intervention, literacy, bilingual/bicultural education, or curriculum theory and development).

18. Work effectively in several types of leadership roles depending on their prior preparation and experience and career objectives (leadership capabilities may be demonstrated in the areas of observation and supervision of student teachers and interns, teaching of undergraduate college students, administration of early childhood programs, advocacy and public policy activity, and/or basic or applied research in early childhood education).

19. Demonstrate understanding of theoretical knowledge in education and allied disciplines.

20. Interpret and expand the knowledge base by completing a dissertation that involves basic or applied research and study.

Preparing an NCATE Folio

If an institution seeking National Council for Accreditation of Teacher Education (NCATE) accreditation offers a program in early childhood education, it must prepare for NAEYC a curriculum folio. NAEYC will review the folio to determine whether or not the program is in compliance with NAEYC's curriculum guidelines for initial and/or advanced programs (see pp. 17–24). In preparing the folio, faculty should keep in mind that their purpose is to clearly and succinctly describe to the reviewer how their program prepares competent and knowledgeable teachers of young children. The amount of information submitted should be sufficient to achieve this purpose.

NCATE and NAEYC define early childhood preparation programs as those that prepare students to work with children from birth through age 8. Preparation of teachers for the primary grades in a traditional elementary-school model should not be labeled early childhood education. Institutions are encouraged to show those programs that follow a traditional elementary-school model as elementary programs rather than early childhood programs.

Instructions for preparing an NCATE Folio should be obtained directly from NCATE. Request *NCATE Approved Curriculum Guidelines,* 2010 Massachusetts Avenue, NW, Suite 500, Washington, DC 20036; 202-466-7496. NCATE provides a cover sheet and matrix form to use in preparing the folio. Programs should use the matrix provided by NCATE to report evidence of compliance with NAEYC's curriculum guidelines.

Here is a list of materials to include in the folio, listed in the order that appears on the cover sheet provided by NCATE.

A. Overview and Scope

This should be a brief description of your program. Please include the structure of the program (four-year, five-year, etc.) and the view of early childhood as defined by the scope of the program (birth to 8, 3 to 5, 3 to 8, etc.).

Objectives of the Program. This is the list of the specific objectives that you expect students to meet as a result of the program.

Course of Studies. Please list all of the courses exactly, including name, prefix, and number, and the order in which students take them in the early childhood professional program. *Indicate all required courses with an asterisk.* (Note: It is helpful to include a student program planning sheet in this section.)

Descriptions of Field Experiences, Student Teaching, and Internships. Please provide a complete description of all field experiences that are required in your program. Include the length of time in each setting, the level (infant/toddler, ages 3 to 5, kindergarten, primary), the geographic location (rural, urban, suburban, lab school, etc.), the type of supervision provided by your institution, the nature of any seminar experiences, and any other distinguishing features, such as the cultural diversity of the settings and the training for cooperating teachers.

Explanation of How the Program May Deviate from the Guidelines. If you feel that your program deviates from the NAEYC guidelines, describe the deviation in complete detail.

Description of where the program is located within the professional education unit and its interrelationships with other programs in the unit and the university/college. Indicate whether your program is housed in a department, school, or other unit. Describe the working relationships that exist with requirements of other departments for general studies, the academic major (if required), and any interdisciplinary program requirements.

List faculty with primary assignments in the early childhood education program. Provide rank, responsibilities, and tenure status for those faculty who have primary teaching assignments in the early childhood program. *Do not send vitae.*

Number of graduates from the program(s) at different levels in each of the past three years. Include the numbers for both Initial and Advanced levels.

Syllabi for post-baccalaureate education courses and the criteria used at admission to determine if the candidate has adequate academic background in the subject to be taught.

B. Matrix

Fill out one matrix for the Initial program and a second matrix for the Advanced program. Include the prefix, course number, and title for each course and reference the page number of the corresponding syllabus. *Please check to ensure that all course numbers are accurate.*

C. Syllabi

Include syllabi for all required courses that are listed in the matrix and any other courses cited as substantially meeting a guideline.

D. Optional items

Please include other information that may help the reviewer understand your program. *Do not send college catalogs, student handbooks, or other lengthy publications.*

Here are some points to remember in preparing the folio for NAEYC reviewers:

- Include the program levels—Initial, Advanced, or both—on the cover of the folio.
- Have one section in the folio for Initial programs and a second section for Advanced programs.
- If submitting a master's program, double-check whether it is Initial or Advanced and that the correct matrix is completed. *The Initial Master's leads to initial licensure for students who do not have a baccalaureate degree in early childhood education. The Advanced Master's provides in-depth education for students who have an academic background in early childhood.*
- Be sure to provide complete information for each section.
- Number the pages in the entire folio and place dividers between the overview, matrix, and syllabi.
- Check that the first item in the folio is the completed cover sheet.
- Remember to include each of the items described above (**A** through **D**) in the folio.

SECTION 2. DEC/CEC PERSONNEL STANDARDS FOR EARLY EDUCATION AND EARLY INTERVENTION: GUIDELINES FOR LICENSURE IN EARLY CHILDHOOD SPECIAL EDUCATION—

RECOMMENDATIONS OF
THE DIVISION FOR EARLY CHILDHOOD/COUNCIL FOR EXCEPTIONAL CHILDREN
THE NATIONAL ASSOCIATION FOR THE EDUCATION OF YOUNG CHILDREN
THE ASSOCIATION OF TEACHER EDUCATORS

RECOMMENDED STANDARDS

Overview

This section contains recommendations for licensure for individuals working as early childhood special educators in a variety of settings serving children at birth through age 8 with special needs and their families. The recommendations have been developed as a part of the ongoing process of clarifying roles and standards for individuals employed in early education and early intervention. These recommendations build upon and extend the prior separate efforts of the Association of Teacher Educators (ATE), the Division for Early Childhood (DEC) of the Council for Exceptional Children, and the National Association for the Education of Young Children (NAEYC) to generate guidelines for licensure in early education and early childhood special education (McCollum et al. 1989; ATE & NAEYC 1991; ATE & NAEYC 1991b; CEC 1992; DEC 1992; ATE, DEC, & NAEYC 1994). The recommendations derived from a commitment to establishing a shared vision among these key professional organizations in early education and early intervention for the credentialing of all individuals working with young children and their families.

This section has several important features. First, the fundamental position of ATE, DEC, and NAEYC that a freestanding credentialing process is required for persons who work with young children, separate from the credentialing of general educators or of special educators, is strongly supported. Elements of existing position statements from these organizations are incorporated and expanded upon in response to current indicators of effective practice. Second, this work offers a conceptual base for identifying the knowledge and skills needed by individuals working with young children, including those with special needs. Third, a framework is provided for clarifying the professional roles in early childhood education and early childhood special education. In particular, the relationship between early childhood educators and early childhood special educators is articulated. Finally, the three organizations describe specific content areas around which to organize the licensing of individuals working as early childhood special educators in a variety of community settings.

The purpose of this concept statement is to provide guidance to states as they develop personnel standards for early childhood special educators. It is intended that these recommendations be reviewed in the context of NAEYC's standards for early childhood educators and guidelines for higher education programs preparing individuals to work with all young children and their families, including those with special needs (see Section 1).

These recommendations should support increased uniformity and unification across states in the preparation, licensure, and practice of early childhood educators and early childhood special educators. However, the recommendations should be seen as flexible enough to be applied to the individual variations in licensure practices and service delivery contexts of each state. Individual states must make decisions about who enters the profession, the length of preservice training, the level at which training must occur, and the degree to which integration of early childhood education and early childhood special education can occur in preparation and licensure.

Specific standards for individuals in related service professions are not articulated here. However, it is the position of ATE, DEC, and NAEYC that all individuals who work with children in early childhood settings must possess, to a degree congruent with their roles, the knowledge and skills for working with young children with special needs (ATE, DEC, & NAEYC 1994). The roles and the unique knowledge and skills required of professionals in related disciplines have been widely discussed (McCollum & Thorp 1988). Further, a compendium of common core competencies as well as some discipline-specific competencies can be found in the other DEC documents (DEC Personnel Committee 1992). It remains the responsibility of each profession to establish these standards and to relate them to state licensure or credentialing processes elsewhere.

Background

There is increasing capacity, nationally, to provide comprehensive, coordinated services for young children with special learning and developmental needs and their families. Federal and state policy initiatives have resulted in more programs for young children in general. With increasing attention to the availability of early education and early intervention services has come recognition of the need to identify standards for practice in providing these services (Bredekamp 1987; DEC Personnel Committee 1992). Further, there is increasing consensus, supported by policy, that the context for service delivery for young children with special needs is the same community setting where their typically developing peers are found. Finally, there is increasing recognition that the changing nature of services to young children requires examination of personnel preparation practices (McCollum & Thorp 1988; Miller 1992; Stayton & Miller 1993). Examination is needed of (a) the structure for licensing individuals who will work in early education and early intervention and (b) the relationship between early childhood education and early childhood special education, which often have been seen as separate fields (Burton et al. 1992; Bredekamp 1993).

This statement of recommendations has been developed as a result of a consensus-building process among the ATE, DEC, and NAEYC. It evolved as a result of informal conversations between these professional organizations in recognition of their overlapping interests in ensuring high-quality environments for all young children, including those with special needs. It is an extension of a position statement cooperatively developed by all three organizations, presented for feedback and review to their respective memberships, and approved during 1993-94 by each organization's executive board (ATE, DEC, & NAEYC 1994).

These professional organizations have long recognized their roles in recommending standards for credentialing individuals who work with young children. ATE and NAEYC have an approved position on licensure of early childhood teachers (ATE & NAEYC 1991). In 1991 these organizations began the process of developing guidelines for early childhood special educators that would be congruent with this existing position. DEC has an approved position providing recommendations for licensure of early childhood special educators (ATE, DEC, & NAEYC 1994) and has compiled professional competencies for early intervention personnel (DEC Personnel Committee 1992). Furthermore, the Council for Exceptional Children has identified common core knowledge and skills for all special education teachers (CEC 1992) and is engaged in the process of identifying knowledge and skills necessary for teachers to practice within particular specialty areas (CEC 1993). For the specialty area of early childhood special education, DEC's recommendations for licensure will be incorporated in the CEC documents.

Each of these positions has been used in the development of state credentialing standards (Fore 1992; Thorp & Fader 1993). However, there is wide variation in state standards—their existence, the ages of children covered, and the roles and settings to which they apply (NEC*TAS 1992; Bredekamp 1993; Thorp & Fader 1993). Only a few states have adopted licensure standards that demonstrate either a clear relationship between early childhood educators and early childhood special educators or the unification of those fields in a single license (Thorp & Fader 1993). As standards for practice have been clarified (Bredekamp 1987, 1993; Bredekamp &

Rosegrant 1992; DEC Task Force on Recommended Practices 1993), and as children with disabilities receive services in inclusive community settings, it has become clear that there is a need to identify standards to ensure that individuals are available and adequately prepared to work with young children in these new contexts. ATE, DEC, and NAEYC, therefore, acknowledged the need to revisit their current positions and develop a joint position on the qualifications required of all personnel who work with young children, including those with special needs. It is expected that this collaborative process will have several desirable outcomes: (a) the coherence of state credentialing guidelines, including clearer articulation of the roles of early childhood educators and early childhood special educators; (b) congruence between personnel standards and standards of recommended practice in early childhood service delivery; (c) the increased probability that services to young children with disabilities are delivered in the context of services to all young children; and (d) those services are provided by personnel prepared to provide high-quality programs appropriate for all young children.

The recommendations contained in this statement support and expand upon the prior positions of ATE, DEC, and NAEYC. The content of the recommended standards is compatible with that in existing standards. Standards have been elaborated upon, however, to describe outcomes expected of candidates for licensure, to be congruent with categories used in guidelines for the National Council for Accreditation of Teacher Education (NCATE) accreditation of teacher education programs, and to incorporate current conceptions of attributes of high-quality programs. These recommendations were derived from two sources: (a) an analysis of the roles currently necessary to support early education and early intervention for young children with disabilities in inclusive community settings where typically developing young children are also served and (b) an analysis of the relationship between the role of early childhood educators and early childhood special educators in these settings. In an evolving field it is essential to modify recommendations for licensure to address those changes. Similarly, the recommendations provided here will require periodic review and revision.

Conceptual Base Guiding Personnel Recommendations

ATE, DEC, and NAEYC recommend that personnel standards be derived from empirically defensible knowledge and clearly articulated philosophical assumptions about what constitutes effective early education and early intervention for young children with special needs and their families. These areas of consensus represent current recommended practice in the fields of early education and early intervention. This knowledge base and set of philosophical assumptions, in turn, have influenced decisions about the recommended structure and content of certification recommendations.

THE UNIQUENESS OF EARLY CHILDHOOD AS A DEVELOPMENTAL PHASE

Early education and early intervention evolved from a belief that the characteristics of development and learning of young children are different from those of older children and adults. Thus, programs serving young children should be structured to support those unique developmental and learning characteristics. The personnel in early childhood programs should have a thorough understanding of the developmental needs of young children and of strategies for structuring a supportive learning environment responsive to those needs (Cataldo 1984; McCollum et al. 1989; ATE & NAEYC 1991; Carta et al. 1991). Further, personnel working with young children with disabilities must first recognize that these are young children (Wolery, Strain, & Bailey 1992) and then bring to the intervention process an understanding of the interrelationship between the development of young children and the impact of disability on development and subsequent implications for intervention (McCollum et al. 1989; ATE & NAEYC 1991).

For purposes here, early childhood is defined as extending from birth through age 8. This definition has both a theoretical and pragmatic rationale. From a theoretical perspective, development is seen as occurring on a continuum, requiring gradual changes in approaches to instruction as development proceeds (McCollum et al. 1989; ATE & NAEYC 1991). A program serving infants and toddlers will look markedly different from one serving children ages 5 to 8; yet each program will share underlying organizational principles that contrast starkly with programs for older children.

Pragmatically, there are clear benefits to be derived from linking the entire birth-through-8 age range, particularly for the two age extremes—birth to 3 and 5 to 8. Current conceptualizations of effective practice with young children were first proposed as a response to the apparent trend toward downward escalation of curriculum, in particular to the practice of providing formal and academic instruction to young children (Bredekamp 1987; Bredekamp & Rosegrant 1992). In order for children in the early primary grades to be taught in a developmentally appropriate fashion, personnel must be prepared to see the link between child development and teaching strategies uniquely structured to respond to that development.

THE SIGNIFICANT ROLE OF FAMILIES IN EARLY EDUCATION AND INTERVENTION

Families provide the primary context for young children's learning and development. The central role of families suggests the need for establishing relationships with families that ensure continuity between families and the providers of early education and intervention (Powell 1994). These relationships should be built upon mutual support of each other's roles, upon a commitment to joint decision-making, and upon respect for families' choices and preferences for their level of involvement (Vincent et al. 1990; McGonigal, Kaufmann, & Johnson 1991; Harry 1992; Garshelis & McConnell 1993).

The conception of collaboration with families suggests an active role for families, placing them at the center of the educational process if that is their choice (McLean & Odom 1993). It represents a logical evolution of the principles of family involvement that have traditionally characterized early childhood services. Current principles differ from traditional principles in intensity and in an increased focus on engaging families in a mutual relationship via family-centered services rather than as recipients of professional expertise (McGonigal, Kaufmann, & Johnson 1991; Hills 1992; Bredekamp 1993). Furthermore, it reflects recent changes in public policy (Beckman et al. 1991). Part H and, to a lesser extent, Part B of the Individuals with Disabilities Education Act (*IDEA Amendments* 1991) provide roles for families in assessment, planning, and intervention, as well as in the larger system development process. Family concerns and priorities must be addressed, and intervention must be provided in environments that are meaningful for families (Vincent et al. 1990; McGonigal, Kaufmann, & Johnson 1991; Beckman et al. 1993). Professional standards should be developed to ensure effective collaboration with families, derived from (a) an understanding of the experiences of families of young children, including those with disabilities; (b) a knowledge of specific strategies to establish and maintain productive relationships with families with diverse needs, experiences, and preferences; and (c) a knowledge of specific legal requirements (Wolery, Strain, & Bailey 1992; Beckman et al. 1993).

THE ROLE OF DEVELOPMENTALLY AND INDIVIDUALLY APPROPRIATE PRACTICES

Developmentally appropriate practices provide a framework for instructional practices based on the assumption that the opportunities needed for learning and development come primarily from children's active engagement and participation in their environment (Bredekamp 1987). Thus, developmentally appropriate practices maximize children's opportunities to make choices, value children's interests, and emphasize play and enjoyment. Developmentally appropriate practices encompass practices that are both age appropriate and individually appropriate. Age-appropriate programs provide for a wide range of interests and abilities within which the chronological-age expectation of a typically developing child can be found. Individually appropriate planning is guided by an understanding of the needs and interests of individual children and of the adaptations that may be necessary to enhance learning.

There has been much discussion of the applicability of developmentally appropriate practices to early childhood special education (Carta et al. 1991; Mallory 1992; Bredekamp 1993; Carta et al. 1993; McLean & Odom 1993; McCollum & Bair 1994). Children with and without special needs have been found to be more actively involved in activities they initiate themselves in contrast to teacher-initiated activities (Diamond, Hestenes, & O'Connor 1994). However, achieving a broad enough conception of developmentally appropriate practices that are truly relevant for all young children, including those with special needs, remains a challenge. For example, when planning for young children with severe disabilities, chronological-age appropriate practices may differ markedly from developmental-age appropriate practices. Yet, in many instances the former are necessary for successful inclusion and for the functional development of that child (McLean & Odom 1993). Furthermore, teacher behavior might best be viewed as occurring on a continuum from highly directive to facilitatively instructional behaviors (Bredekamp & Rosegrant 1992). In judging the degree of support needed by an individual child, it seems critical first to err on the side of less-directive strategies and then when planning for lesser or greater degrees of support to consider what is known about the capacity of an individual child to obtain feedback from the environment and from peers (Bredekamp & Rosegrant 1992; Johnson & Johnson 1992; Bredekamp 1993; McCollum & Bair 1994). Finally, individually appropriate practices for young children with special needs require active assessing and planning for individual children. Such planning is based upon strengths, needs, and a clear understanding of environmental adaptations that may be necessary for that child to benefit from the environment.

Personnel standards for the early childhood special educator should ensure skillful application of developmentally appropriate practices with all young children and especially those with special needs. Therefore, standards must address the key dimensions of the continuum of teaching strategies; understanding the role of the child, the role of the environment, the behavioral expectations of typically developing peers, and the role of the professional.

THE PREFERENCE FOR SERVICE DELIVERY IN INCLUSIVE SETTINGS

Young children with special needs are increasingly receiving services in integrated settings along with their typically developing peers. Both Part B and Part H of the IDEA Amendments (1991) support early intervention and education in inclusive settings. Specifically, infants and toddlers must receive services in normalized, natural environments, and preschoolers with special needs must receive services in the least restrictive environment. The regulations for Part H define natural environments as "settings that are natural and normal for the child's age peers who have no disability," including home and community settings. Based on the least-restrictive-environment principle, states must ensure that

To the maximum extent appropriate, children with disabilities, including children in public or private institutions and other care facilities, are educated with children who are not disabled, and that special classes, separate schooling, or other removal of children with disabilities from the regular education environment occurs only when the nature or severity of the disability is such that education in regular classes with the use of supplementary aids and services cannot be achieved satisfactorily. (*IDEA Amendments* 1991, 606 [USC Code 1412])

DEC and NAEYC (1993) identified inclusion as the preferred service delivery option for young children with special needs. This practice of inclusion is based on the belief that young children with special needs are more similar to their peers than different from them and that all young children benefit from learning together as members of a diverse community. The strength of the movement to provide services to young children in normalized community settings provides the incentive for developing a unified statement on professional standards.

Because inclusion is the preferred option, all professionals working with young children need to be sufficiently knowledgeable about the needs of young children with disabilities and about appropriate interventions with them in order to provide age-appropriate and individually appropriate services to all of the children with whom they work. Professionals must also be prepared to work in the diverse range of community settings in which young children and families receive services. Some professionals now argue that for the full inclusion of infants, toddlers, and preschoolers with special needs to occur, personnel preparation programs should combine early childhood and early childhood special education (Odom & McEvoy 1990; Bredekamp 1992; Burton et al. 1992; Miller 1992). In addition, a commitment to inclusionary practices requires the delineation of a range of roles from early childhood educator to early childhood special educator as well as a delineation of professional standards for these roles.

THE IMPORTANCE OF CULTURALLY COMPETENT PROFESSIONAL BEHAVIOR

All development and learning occurs within and is influenced by a cultural context. Because of the great diversity within our communities and among and within families, professionals working with young children should be prepared to provide culturally competent services. Arcia, Keyes, Gallagher, and Herrick (1993) reported that approximately 32% of children under age 5 in the United States are of ethnic minority. In some states this percentage is approaching or has already reached majority status. Research suggests, however, that the majority of early interventionists are Caucasian (Christensen 1992). Whereas, African Americans are relatively well represented in the staff of the early childhood programs (Kisker et al. 1991), they remain the minority of total staff. With this discrepancy between the cultural and ethnic status of consumers and providers of services,

it is imperative that specific knowledge and skills be articulated to enable individuals working with young children and families to approach diversity in an effective manner within the context of the service delivery setting.

P.L.102-119 extended services to typically underserved groups, including cultural and ethnic minority groups, by requiring states to develop policies and practices with families that ensure access to culturally competent services within the community. Roberts defined cultural competence as "a set of congruent behaviors, attitudes, and policies that come together in a system, agency, or among professionals to enable that system, agency, or those professionals to work effectively in crosscultural situations" (1990, 15). Recommended practices for personnel competence indicate that cultural and ethnic diversity must be addressed in both didactic program content and through field experiences to prepare professionals to respect the diversity of cultures found in a community through intervention practices and policies (DEC Task Force on Recommended Practices 1993). To work effectively with culturally diverse families, professionals must be knowledgeable about their own cultural background and acquire general knowledge of specific cultures, including their beliefs about disability and child-rearing practices; and professionals must be aware of the verbal and nonverbal communication styles used in various cultural contexts, understand how their own cultural beliefs and values have an impact on their interactions with families, and be aware of the impact of policies and practices upon children and families from cultural and ethnic minority groups (Hanson, Lynch, & Wayman 1990; Christensen 1992; Lynch & Hanson 1992).

THE IMPORTANCE OF COLLABORATIVE INTERPERSONAL AND INTERPROFESSIONAL ACTIONS

With the implementation of family-centered services and the inclusion of young children with special needs in general community settings, personnel need to be able to work collaboratively with family members, with others in their own discipline, and with individuals from other disciplines as members of teams. The IDEA Amendments (1991) have provided states with regulations supporting collaboration among disciplines and with families. This shift in service delivery has resulted in the need for early childhood special educators to adjust their roles from the primary role of direct service provider to one of more indirect service delivery (such as consultant, technical assistant, and staff development specialist) (File & Kontos 1992; Buysse & Wesley 1993).

In service delivery roles that are even more indirect, the early childhood special educator must possess knowledge and skills required for direct service delivery to consult effectively with colleagues who work on an ongoing basis with children and families. In addition, early childhood special educators must develop skills in building interpersonal relationships, communicating with early childhood educators and related services professionals, and providing technical assistance/training to others (File & Kontos 1992; Buysse & Wesley 1993). It is also imperative that the early childhood special educator be knowledgeable about the philosophical base, methodological approaches, and terminology of the disciplines with which collaboration/consultation occurs (McCollum & Thorp 1988; File & Kontos 1992). The need for this type of knowledge provides a rationale for interdisciplinary preservice training programs. The interagency organization of early childhood services within communities also establishes a rationale for interdisciplinary preservice programs that effectively prepare professionals for collaborative roles.

A Framework for Clarifying Professional Roles

Individuals who work with children in early childhood settings must possess, to a degree congruent with their roles, the knowledge and skills for working with young children with special learning and developmental needs and their families. Personnel standards must support the practice of inclusion, the provision of services for young children with special needs in general early childhood programs and other community-based settings in which typically developing young children are also served. Personnel standards should also support the trend toward the development of early childhood/early childhood special education teacher training programs and state licensure that incorporates all recommended personnel standards from DEC and NAEYC. These personnel standards are necessary for individuals functioning in a variety of roles, including but not limited to (a) early childhood educators, (b) early childhood special educators, and (c) related-services professionals.

EARLY CHILDHOOD EDUCATOR

Early childhood educators should possess a common core of knowledge and skills that includes content specific to young children, birth through age 8, both with and without disabilities. This content includes child development and learning, curriculum development and implementation, family and community relationships, assessment and evaluation, and professionalism with appropriate field experiences through which to apply this content. The early childhood educator may work directly with children birth through age 8, including children with a range of abilities and special needs, and work collaboratively with families and other professionals. This work may occur in a variety of settings, such as public and private schools and centers, homes, and other facilities in which children within this age range and their families are served. In addition to the traditional role of teacher, the early childhood educator may assume a variety of roles that require specialized knowledge and skills, including but not limited to early childhood subject-area teacher, parent education coordinator, social service coordinator, education coordinator, program administrator, and early childhood unit administrator (NAEYC 1992, 1994).

EARLY CHILDHOOD SPECIAL EDUCATOR

Early childhood special educators should also possess, with the early childhood educator, a common core of knowledge and skills as well as specialized knowledge and skills regarding young children birth through age 8 with special needs and their families. This content includes child development and learning, curriculum development and implementation, family and community relationships, assessment and evaluation, and professionalism with appropriate field experiences through which to apply this content. The early childhood special educator may work directly with children with special needs who are in this age range or work in a collaborative relationship with early childhood educators, family members and other professionals serving young children with special learning and developmental needs and their families. The early childhood special educator may provide services in both public and private schools and centers, homes, hospitals, and other facilities in which young children and their families are served. Bricker (1989) discussed five major roles for early childhood special educators: conceptualizer, synthesizer, instructor, evaluator, and listener. The conceptualizer has a broad conceptual knowledge base of developmental processes and curricular domains. This broad conceptual base allows for flexibility in adapting for children with special needs. The synthesizer actively seeks input from other professionals and coordinates this information in planning programs and service delivery strategies for children and families. The instructor role encompasses direct work with children who have special needs, collaboration with families, and training for ancillary program staff. The evaluator develops an evaluation system that assesses outcomes of children and families and provides mechanisms for reporting to staff. The listener role is a support role for the family. It includes communication skills, such as listening, questioning, and problem solving.

In an investigation of roles across 10 disciplines, Bailey (1989) identified roles specific to early interventionists with a special education background. These roles are to (a) assess children's development; (b) plan intervention programs; (c) implement intervention services; (d) coordinate interdisciplinary services; (e) follow through with recommendations from consultants; (f) assess family resources, priorities, and concerns; (g) plan and implement services for families; (h) coordinate interagency services; (i) conduct program evaluation; and (j) serve as an advocate for children and families. Although delineated differently, it seems that the roles Bailey specified identify activities that can be subsumed under the broader conceptual role categories described by Bricker (1989) and can serve as a foundation for the content in these professional guidelines. It also seems apparent that these role categories are very similar to those assumed by the early childhood educator. Differences in the early childhood educator and early childhood special educator's roles arise, however, when one examines the manner and degree to which educators implement each role. For example, the early childhood educator's primary roles in conducting assessment may be in screening or in using informal procedures such as observation; whereas the early childhood special educator performs those assessment activities and, in addition, conducts diagnostic assessment, employing criterion-referenced measures for instructional programming, and synthesizes results into written reports.

As discussed earlier, with the shift in service delivery toward family-centered services and inclusion, the early childhood special educator is being required to shift roles from that of primarily providing direct services to indirect service delivery. When direct services are provided by the early childhood special educator, they are likely to be delivered within an inclusion model as a team member (e.g., team teaching) or as a lead teacher, serving children both with and without special needs (i.e., reverse mainstreaming). Indirect service delivery roles continue to require the early childhood special educator to possess knowledge and skills in the roles identified by Bailey (1989) and Bricker (1989) to serve effectively as a consultant, collaborator, parent educator, program administrator, and staff development specialist for family members, other professionals, and paraprofessionals. In states that have adopted unified licensure requirements, the early childhood special educator should be a key team member who will typically assume more indirect service delivery roles, such as consulting/collaborating with early childhood educators and related-services professionals, to ensure appropriate services for young children with special needs and their families.

RELATED-SERVICES PROFESSIONALS

Related-services professionals represent a variety of professional disciplines (e.g., physical therapy, occupational therapy, speech/language pathology, nursing, social work); they provide consultation and support to families and other professionals as well as direct services for children birth through age 8 with special needs. Related-services professionals should also possess a common core of knowledge and skills specific to young children with special needs and their families, along with specialized knowledge and skills in their own professional disciplines.

Structure of Recommended Early Childhood
Special Education Licensure

It is the intention of ATE, DEC, and NAEYC (1994) to provide a framework for personnel standards that is sufficiently flexible to allow states to plan within the context of local limitations, while also maintaining content congruence (ATE & NAEYC 1991) with the philosophy and assumptions discussed previously in this paper. In developing a structure for licensure standards, the following actions are recommended.

1. State agencies should develop freestanding standards for licensure; that is, they should separate from existing general education elementary or secondary licenses and from existing elementary or secondary special education licenses (ATE, DEC, & NAEYC 1994). This recommendation is based on the professional recognition that both early childhood and early childhood special education have distinctive knowledge bases that should drive the preparation of personnel for those fields (McCollum et al. 1989; ATE, DEC, & NAEYC 1994). These licensure standards should apply to all individuals who work with young children with special needs and their families, including early childhood educators, early childhood special educators, and related-services professionals.

2. These licensure standards should encompass birth through age 8 as the early childhood developmental period. Arguments have been made for entirely separate credentialing and training for those working with infants and toddlers. However, the most current regulations for Part H and Part B of P.L. 102-119 appear to lend support to avoiding an artificial demarcation between birth-through-age-3 versus age-3-through-5 licensure by adopting a more seamless perspective on services to young children. The legislation includes attention to transition and continued use of the IFSP (Individual Family Service Plan) throughout the preschool years. Linking the personnel requirements of Part H and Part B at the state level should ensure a commonality of philosophy and practices that would enable more seamless transitions between Part H and Part B services. This broad approach to defining early childhood should minimize implementation problems; enhance the possibility of mobility between roles, settings, and children served; and ensure that professionals are prepared to serve the children and families they are employed to serve. At the same time, recognizing that it is difficult to prepare individuals in a preservice program to be competent across the entire birth-through-8 age range, licensure standards should support age-related subspecialties within a broader licensure pattern that may include at least two adjacent age spans (i.e., infant/toddler and preprimary or preprimary and primary-school age).

3. Reciprocal licensure agreements across states should be developed to ensure the easy mobility of personnel and to ensure uniform standards. Reciprocal licensure agreements imply both age and content congruence across the United States.

4. Separate licenses for the early childhood educator and early childhood special educator should be clearly linked so as to encourage professional mobility between roles. This suggests the development of a career lattice (Bredekamp & Willer 1992) within states that supports not only the upward mobility of professionals within a system but also the horizontal movement of professionals from one setting to another (e.g., Head Start to public school to child care), with comparable responsibilities and compensation. The linkage of separate licensures also supports the option for unified early childhood/early childhood special education personnel preparation programs.

Content Standards for
Early Childhood Special Education Licensure

Licensure standards for the early childhood special educator must articulate the common core of knowledge and skills required for all persons who work with young children with special needs and their families as well as specialization knowledge and skills. The common core of knowledge and skills should be derived from the fields of early childhood education, early childhood special education, and special education, with the specialization knowledge and skills based on the knowledge base from early childhood special education. The content of licensure standards must be congruent with the philosophy and assumptions identified in this statement and reflect the spirit and letter of federal regulations specific to serving young children with special needs and their families. Further, licensure standards should be performance based rather than course based. They should ensure that personnel possess the knowledge and skills to work collaboratively as members of family-professional teams in planning and implementing services for young children with special needs in diverse community settings. Specifically, knowledge and skills should be demonstrated in the areas of (a) child development and learning, (b) curriculum development and implementation, (c) family and community relationships, (d) assessment and evaluation, and (e) professionalism. Application of knowledge and skills should be demonstrated through diverse field experiences.

Licensure standards should reflect the importance of ongoing professional development within state standards. Preservice training should focus on entry-level competence in two age spans of the birth-through-8 age range. To become more competent in these subspecialties, to achieve competence in the full age range, or to specialize in a content or ability area, further training is necessary. Licensure standards, therefore, should recognize that graduate-level training is a desirable component of a career lattice for all professionals working with young children with special needs and seeking greater degrees of specialization in early childhood development and service delivery.

GUIDELINES FOR PREPARATION OF EARLY CHILDHOOD SPECIAL EDUCATION PROFESSIONALS

The competent early childhood special educator demonstrates a common core of knowledge and skills for working with young children with special needs and their families as well as specialization knowledge and skills in at least two of the age subspecialties. The following guidelines describe the specific standards required for the common core and the specialization. These guidelines apply to entry-level licensure whether the training is acquired at the undergraduate or graduate level. These guidelines reflect the philosophy and assumptions discussed previously in this statement and are based on recommended practices derived from theory and research. The guidelines also imply that faculty and supervisors in training programs will be qualified in the area(s) for which they are providing training and supervision. To promote consistency with the NAEYC Guidelines for Preparation of Early Childhood Professionals (Section 1) and to facilitate states using the option to develop combined certifications, the performance standards include the categories of (a) child development and learning, (b) curriculum development and implementation, (c) family and community relationships, (d) assessment and evaluation, (e) professionalism, and (f) field experiences.

Guidelines for Four- and Five-Year Institutions
(Initial Licensure)

1. Child Development and Learning. Programs prepare early childhood special educators to

1.1 Apply theories of child development, both typical and atypical, and apply current research with emphasis on cognitive, motor, social-emotional, communication, adaptive, and aesthetic development in learning situations and family and community contexts.

1.2 Identify pre-, peri-, and postnatal development and factors, such as biological and environmental conditions, that affect children's development and learning.

1.3 Identify specific disabilities, including the etiology, characteristics, and classification of common disabilities in young children, and describe specific implications for development and learning in the first years of life.

1.4 Apply knowledge of cultural and linguistic diversity and the significance of sociocultural and political contexts for development and learning and recognize that children are best understood in the contexts of family, culture, and society.

1.5 Demonstrate understanding of (a) developmental consequences of stress and trauma, (b) protective factors and resilience, (c) the development of mental health, and (d) the importance of supportive relationships.

2. Curriculum Development and Implementation. Programs prepare early childhood special educators to

2.1 Plan and implement developmentally and individually appropriate curricula and instructional practices based on knowledge of individual children, the family, the community, and curricula goals and content through the following actions:

2.1.1 make specific adaptations for the special needs of children who have unique talents, learning and developmental needs, or specific disabilities;

2.1.2 develop an Individual Family Service Plan (IFSP) or Individual Education Plan (IEP), incorporating both child and family outcomes, in partnership with family members and other professionals;

2.1.3 incorporate information and strategies from multiple disciplines in the design of intervention strategies;

2.1.4 design plans that incorporate the use of technology, including adaptive and assistive technology;

2.1.5 develop and select learning experiences and strategies that affirm and respect family, cultural, and societal diversity, including language differences;

2.1.6 plan for and link current developmental and learning experiences and teaching strategies with those of the next educational setting;

2.1.7 select intervention curricula and methods for children with specific disabilities including motor, sensory, health, communication, social-emotional, and cognitive disabilities;

2.1.8 support and facilitate family and child interactions as primary contexts for learning and development;

2.1.9 implement developmentally and functionally appropriate individual and group activities using a variety of formats, including play, environmental routines, parent-mediated activities, small-group projects, cooperative learning, inquiry experiences, and systematic instruction;

2.1.10 develop and implement an integrated curriculum that focuses on children's needs and interests and takes into account culturally valued content and children's home experiences;

2.1.11 select, develop, and evaluate developmentally and functionally appropriate materials, equipment, and environments;

2.1.12 demonstrate appropriate use of technology, including adaptive and assistive technology; and

2.1.13 employ pedagogically sound and legally defensible instructional practices.

2.2 Use individual and group guidance and problem-solving techniques to develop positive and supportive relationships with children, to encourage and teach positive social skills and interaction among children, to promote positive strategies of conflict resolution, and to develop personal self-control, self-motivation, and self-esteem by the following means:

2.2.1 select and implement methods of behavior support and management appropriate for young children with special needs, including a range of strategies from less-directive, less-structured methods (e.g., verbal support and modeling) to more-directive, more-structured methods (e.g., applied behavior analysis).

2.3 Establish and maintain physically and psychologically safe and healthy learning environments that promote development and learning through the following actions:

2.3.1 provide a stimuli-rich indoor and outdoor environment that employs materials, media, and technology, including adaptive and assistive technology;

2.3.2 organize space, time, peers, materials, and adults to maximize child progress in group and home settings;

2.3.3 implement basic health, nutrition, and safety management practices for young children, including specific procedures for infants and toddlers and procedures regarding childhood illness and communicable diseases;

2.3.4 implement nutrition and feeding strategies for children with special needs;

2.3.5 use appropriate health appraisal procedures and recommend referral and ongoing follow-up to appropriate community health and social services;

2.3.6 identify aspects of medical care for premature, low-birth-weight, and other medically fragile babies, including methods for care of young children dependent on technology, and implications of medical conditions for child development and family resources, concerns, and priorities; and

2.3.7 recognize signs of emotional distress, child abuse, and neglect in young children and follow procedures for reporting known or suspected abuse or neglect to appropriate authorities.

3. Family and Community Relationships. Programs prepare early childhood special educators to

3.1 Establish and maintain positive, collaborative relationships with families in the following ways:

3.1.1 apply family systems theory and knowledge of the dynamics, roles, and relationships within families and communities;

3.1.2 demonstrate sensitivity to differences in family structures and social and cultural backgrounds;

3.1.3 assist families in identifying their resources, priorities, and concerns in relation to their child's development;

3.1.4 respect parents' choices and goals for children and communicate effectively with parents about curriculum and children's progress;

3.1.5 involve families in assessing and planning for individual children, including children with special needs;

3.1.6 implement a range of family-oriented services based on the family's identified resources, priorities, and concerns;

3.1.7 implement family services consistent with due-process safeguards; and

3.1.8 evaluate services with families.

3.2 Collaborate/consult with other professionals and with agencies in the larger community to support children's development, learning, and well-being by the following means:

3.2.1 apply models of team process in diverse service delivery settings;

3.2.2 employ various team membership roles;

3.2.3 identify functions of teams as determined by mandates and service delivery needs of children and families;

3.2.4 identify structures supporting interagency collaboration, including interagency agreements, referral, and consultation;

3.2.5 participate as a team member to identify dynamics of team roles, interaction, communication, team building, problem solving, and conflict resolution;

3.2.6 employ two-way communication skills; and

3.2.7 evaluate and design processes and strategies that support transitions between hospital, home, and infant/toddler, preprimary, and primary programs.

3.3 Administer, supervise, and consult with/instruct other adults by the following actions:

3.3.1 employ adult-learning principles in supervising and training other adults;

3.3.2 facilitate the identification of staff development needs and strategies for professional growth;

3.3.3 apply various models of consultation in diverse settings;

3.3.4 provide consultation and training in content areas specific to services for children and families and organization/development of programs; and

3.3.5 provide feedback and evaluate performance in collaboration with other adults.

4. Assessment and Evaluation. Programs prepare early childhood special educators to

4.1 Assess children's cognitive, social-emotional, communication, motor, adaptive, and aesthetic development by the following means:

4.1.1 select and use a variety of informal and formal assessment instruments and procedures, including observational methods, to make decisions about children's learning and development;

4.1.2 select and administer assessment instruments and procedures based on the purpose of the assessment being conducted and in compliance with established criteria and standards;

4.1.3 develop and use authentic, performance-based assessments of children's learning to assist in planning, to communicate with children and parents, and to engage children in self-assessment;

4.1.4 involve families as active participants in the assessment process;

4.1.5 participate and collaborate as a team member with other professionals in conducting family-centered assessments;

4.1.6 communicate assessment results and integrate assessment results from others as an active team participant in the development and implementation of the IEP and IFSP;

4.1.7 monitor, summarize, and evaluate the acquisition of child and family outcomes as outlined on the IFSP or IEP;

4.1.8 select, adapt, and administer assessment instruments and procedures for specific sensory and motor disabilities;

4.1.9 communicate options for programs and services at the next level and assist the family in planning for transition; and

4.1.10 implement culturally unbiased assessment instruments and procedures.

4.2 Develop and use formative and summative program evaluation to ensure comprehensive quality of the total environment for children, families, and the community.

5. Professionalism. Programs prepare early childhood special education professionals to

5.1 Articulate the historical, philosophical, and legal basis of services for young children both with and without special needs.

5.2 Identify ethical and policy issues related to educational, social, and medical services for young children and their families.

5.3 Identify current trends and issues in the fields of early childhood education, early childhood special education, and special education.

5.4 Identify legislation that affects children, families, and programs for children.

5.5 Adhere to the profession's Code of Ethical Conduct.

5.6 Serve as advocates on behalf of young children and their families, improved quality of programs and services for young children, and enhanced professional status and working conditions for early childhood special educators.

5.7 Reflect upon his/her own professional practice and develop, implement, and evaluate a professional development plan.

5.8 Participate actively in professional organizations.

5.9 Read and critically apply research and recommended practices.

6. Field Experiences. Programs prepare early childhood special educators by having them

6.1 Observe and participate under the supervision of qualified professionals in a variety of settings in which young children with special needs from birth through age 8 and their families are served (e.g., homes, public and private centers, schools, community agencies).

6.2 Work effectively with children of diverse ages (i.e., infants, toddlers, preschoolers, primary-school age), with children with diverse abilities, with children reflecting culturally and linguistically diverse family systems.

6.3 Participate under supervision as an interagency and intraagency team member.

6.4 Provide consultation services under supervision.

6.5 Demonstrate ability to work effectively during supervised student teaching and/or intensive, ongoing practica experiences (totaling at least 300 clock hours) in at least two different settings, serving children of two different age groups (i.e., infant/toddler, preprimary, or primary school) and with varying abilities.

6.6 Analyze and evaluate field experiences, including supervised experience in working with families and other professionals.

REFERENCES

Arcia, E., L. Keyes, J.J. Gallagher, & H. Herrick. 1993. National portrait of sociodemographic factors associated with underutilization of services: Relevance to early intervention. *Journal of Early Intervention* 17 (3): 283–97.

Association of Teacher Educators, & National Association for the Education of Young Children (ATE & NAEYC). 1991. Early childhood teacher certification. *Young Children* 47 (1): 16–21.

Association of Teacher Educators, Division for Early Childhood, & National Association for the Education of Young Children (ATE, DEC, & NAEYC). 1994. *Position statement: Personnel standards for early education and early intervention*. Reston, VA: DEC/Council for Exceptional Children.

Bailey, D.B. 1989. Issues and directions in preparing professionals to work with young handicapped children and their families. In *Policy implementation and PL 99-457: Planning for young children with special needs,* eds. J.J. Gallagher, P.L. Trohanis, & R.M. Clifford, 97–132. Baltimore: Paul H. Brookes.

Beckman, P.J., S. Newcomb, N. Frank, L. Brown, & J. Filer. 1993. Providing support to families of infants with disabilities. *Journal of Early Intervention* 17 (4): 445–54.

Bredekamp, S. 1987. *Developmentally appropriate practice in early childhood programs serving children from birth through age 8*. Rev. ed. Washington, DC: NAEYC.

Bredekamp, S. 1992. The early childhood profession coming together. *Young Children* 47 (6): 36–39.

Bredekamp, S. 1993. The relationship between early childhood education and early childhood special education: Healthy marriage or family feud. *Topics in Early Childhood Special Education* 13 (3): 258–73.

Bredekamp, S., & T. Rosegrant, eds. 1992. *Reaching potentials: Appropriate curriculum and assessment for young children,* volume 1. Washington, DC: NAEYC.

Bredekamp, S., & B. Willer. 1992. Of ladders and lattices, cores and cones: Conceptualizing an early childhood professional development system. *Young Children* 47 (3): 47–50.

Bricker, D.B. 1989. *Early intervention for at-risk and handicapped infants, toddlers, and preschool children*. Palo Alto, CA: VORT.

Burton, C.B., A.H. Hains, M.F. Hanline, M. Mclean, & K. McCormick. 1992. Early childhood intervention and education: The urgency for professional unification. *Topics in Early Childhood Special Education* 11 (4): 53–69.

Buysse, V., & P.W. Wesley. 1993. The identity crisis in early childhood special education: A call for professional role clarification. *Topics in Early Childhood Special Education* 13 (4): 418–29.

Carta, J.J., J.B. Atwater, I.S. Schwartz, & S.R. McConnell. 1993. Developmentally appropriate practices and early childhood special education: A reaction to Johnson and McChesney Johnson. *Topics in Early Childhood Special Education* 13 (3): 243–54.

Carta, J.J., I.S. Schwartz, J.B. Atwater, & S.R. McConnell. 1991. Developmentally appropriate practice: Appraising its usefulness for young children with disabilities. *Topics in Early Childhood Special Education* 11 (1): 1–20.

Cataldo, C.Z. 1984. Infant-toddler education: Blending the best approaches. *Young Children* 39 (2): 25–32.

Christensen, C.M. 1992. Multicultural competencies in early intervention: Training professionals for a pluralistic society. *Infants and Young Children* 4 (3): 49–63.

Council for Exceptional Children (CEC). 1992. *Common core of knowledge and skills essential for all beginning special education teachers*. Reston, VA: Author.

Council for Exceptional Children (CEC). 1993. Unpublished communication to Division Presidents from CEC Subcommittee on Knowledge and Skills, 12 January.

Diamond, K.E., L.L. Hestenes, & C.E. O'Connor. 1994. Research in review. Integrating young children with disabilities in preschool: Problems and promise. *Young Children* 4 (2): 68–75.

Division for Early Childhood (DEC) Personnel Committee. 1992. *Compilation of professional competencies for early intervention personnel*. Denver, CO: Author.

Division for Early Childhood (DEC) Task Force on Recommended Practices. 1993. *DEC recommended practices: Indicators of quality in programs for infants and young children with special needs and their families*. Reston, VA: Council for Exceptional Children.

Division for Early Childhood, & the National Association for the Education of Young Children (DEC &

NAEYC). 1993. *Position on inclusion*. Reston, VA: DEC/Council for Exceptional Children.

File, N., & S. Kontos. 1992. Indirect service delivery through consultation: Review and implications for early intervention. *Journal of Early Intervention* 16 (3): 221–33.

Fore, L. 1992. *The relationship between professional recommendations, certification standards and preservice program requirements in early childhood special education*. Ph.D. diss., The College of William and Mary, Williamsburg, Virginia.

Garshelis, J.A., & S.R. McConnell. 1993. Comparison of family needs assessed by mothers, individual professionals, and interdisciplinary teams. *Journal of Early Intervention* 17 (1): 36–49.

Hanson, M., E. Lynch, & K. Wayman. 1990. Honoring cultural diversity of families when gathering data. *Topics in Early Childhood Special Education* 10 (2): 112–31.

Harry, B. 1992. *Cultural diversity, families and the special education system: Communication and empowerment*. New York: Teachers College Press.

Hills, T. 1992. Reaching potentials through appropriate assessment. In *Reaching potentials: Appropriate curriculum and assessment for young children, volume 1*, eds. S. Bredekamp & T. Rosegrant, 43–63. Washington, DC: NAEYC.

Individuals with Disabilities Education Act (IDEA) Amendments of 1991. U.S. Public Law 102-119, Title 20. *U.S. Statutes at Large* 105: 587–608.

Johnson, J.E., & K.M. Johnson. 1992. Clarifying the developmental perspective in response to Carta, Schwartz, Atwater, and McConnell. *Topics in Early Childhood Special Education* 12 (4): 439–57.

Kisker, E.E., S.L. Hofferth, D.A. Phillips, & E. Farquhar. 1991. *A profile of child care settings: Early education and care in 1990*. Washington, DC: U.S. Government Printing Office.

Lynch, E.W., & M.J. Hanson. 1992. *Developing cross-cultural competence: A guide for working with young children and their families*. Baltimore: Paul H. Brookes.

Mallory, B.L. 1992. Is it always appropriate to be developmental? *Topics in Early Childhood Special Education* 11 (4): 1–12.

McCollum, J.A., & H. Bair. 1994. Research in parent-child interaction: Guidance to developmentally appropriate practice for young children with disabilities. In *Diversity and developmentally appropriate practices*, eds. B.L. Mallory & R.S. New, 84–106. New York: Teachers College Press.

McCollum, J., & E. Thorp. 1988. Training of infant specialists: A look to the future. *Infants and Young Children* 1 (2): 55–65.

McCollum, J., M. McLean, K. McCartan, S. Odom, & C. Kaiser. 1989. Recommendations for certification of early childhood special educators. *Journal of Early Intervention* 13 (3): 195–211.

McGonigal, M.J., R.K. Kaufmann, & B.H. Johnson, eds. 1991. *Guidelines and recommended practices for the individualized family service plan*. 2d ed. Bethesda, MD: Association for the Care of Children's Health.

McLean, M.E., & S.L. Odom. 1993. Practices for young children with and without disabilities: A comparison of DEC and NAEYC identified practices. *Topics in Early Childhood Special Education* 13 (3): 274–92.

Miller, P.S. 1992. Segregated programs of teacher education in early childhood: Immoral and inefficient practice. *Topics in Early Childhood Special Education* 11 (4): 39–52.

NAEYC. 1992. NAEYC model of early childhood professional development. In *National Institute for Early Childhood Professional Development: Background materials for working sessions*. Washington, DC: Author.

NAEYC. 1994. *NAEYC guidelines for preparation of early childhood professionals*. Washington, DC: Author.

National Early Childhood Technical Assistance System (NEC*TAS). 1992. *Section 619 profile, May 1992*. Chapel Hill, NC: Author.

Odom, S.L., & M.A. McEvoy. 1990. Mainstreaming at the preschool level: Barriers and tasks for the field. *Topics in Early Childhood Special Education* 10 (2): 48–61.

Powell, D.R. 1994. Parents, pluralism, and the NAEYC statement on developmentally appropriate practice. In *Diversity and developmentally appropriate practices*, eds. B.L. Mallory & R.S. New, 166–82. New York: Teachers College Press.

Roberts, R.N. 1990. *Developing culturally competent programs for families of children with special needs*. Washington, DC: Georgetown University Child Development Center.

Stayton, V.D., & P.S. Miller. 1993. Combining general and special early childhood education standards in personnel preparation programs: Experiences from two states. *Topics in Early Childhood Special Education* 13 (3): 372–87.

Thorp, E.K., & L. Fader. 1993. Summary of state certification standards for early childhood and early childhood special education. Unpublished manuscript.

Vincent, L.J., C.L. Salisbury, P. Strain, C. McCormick, & A. Tessier. 1990. A behavioral-ecological approach to early intervention: Focus on cultural diversity. In *Handbook of early childhood intervention*, eds. S.J. Meisels & J.P. Shonkoff, 173–95. Cambridge: Cambridge University Press.

Wolery, M., P.S. Strain, & D.B. Bailey. 1992. Reaching potentials of children with special needs. In *Reaching potentials: Appropriate curriculum and assessment for young children, volume 1*, eds. S. Bredekamp & T. Rosegrant, 92–111. Washington, DC: NAEYC.

For Further Reading

Atwater, J.B., J.J. Carta, I.S Schwartz, & S.R. McConnell. 1994. Blending developmentally appropriate practice and early childhood special education. In *Diversity and developmentally appropriate practices,* eds. B.L. Mallory & R.S. New, 185–201. New York: Teachers College Press.

Bowman, B. 1992. Reaching potentials of minority children through developmentally and culturally appropriate programs. In *Reaching potentials: Appropriate curriculum and assessments for young children,* volume 1, eds. S. Bredekamp & T. Rosegrant, 128–36. Washington, DC: NAEYC.

Bruder, M.B., R. Anderson, G. Schultz, & M. Caldera. 1991. Project profile: Minos Especales Program: A culturally sensitive early intervention model. *Journal of Early Intervention* 15 (3): 268–77.

Cavallaro, C.C., M. Haney, & B. Cabello. 1993. Developmentally appropriate strategies for promoting full participation in early childhood settings. *Topics in Early Childhood Special Education* 13 (3): 293–307.

Demchak, M., & S. Drinkwater. 1992. Preschoolers with severe disabilities: The case against segregation. *Topics in Early Childhood Special Education* 11 (4): 70–83.

Derman-Sparks, L. 1992. Reaching potentials through anti-bias, multicultural curriculum. In *Reaching potentials: Appropriate curriculum and assessment for young children,* volume 1, eds. S. Bredekamp & T. Rosegrant, 114–27. Washington, DC: NAEYC.

Derman-Sparks, L. 1993. Revisiting multicultural education: What children need to live in a diverse society. *Dimensions of Early Childhood* 21 (2): 6–9.

Derman-Sparks, L., & the A.B.C. Task Force. 1989. *Anti-bias curriculum: Tools for empowering young children.* Washington, DC: NAEYC.

Fenichel, E.S., & L. Eggbeer. 1990. *Preparing practitioners to work with infants, toddlers and their families: Issues and recommendations for educators and trainers.* Arlington, VA: National Center for Clinical Infant Programs.

Friend, M., & L. Cook. 1992. *Interactions: Collaboration skills for school professionals.* New York: Logmans.

Genishi, C., A.H. Dyson, & R. Fassler. 1994. Language and diversity in early childhood: Whose voices are appropriate? In *Diversity and developmentally appropriate practices,* eds. B.L. Mallory & R.S. New, 250–68. New York: Teachers College Press.

Golin, A.K., & A.J. Ducanis. 1981. *The interdisciplinary team: A handbook for the education of exceptional children.* Rockville, MD: Aspen.

Johnson, K.M., & J.E. Johnson. 1993. Rejoinder to Carta, Atwater, Schwartz, and McConnell. *Topics in Early Childhood Special Education* 13 (3): 255–57.

Jones, E., & L. Derman-Sparks. 1992. Meeting the challenge of diversity. *Young Children* 47 (2): 12–18.

Kagan, S.L., & A.M. Rivera. 1991. Collaboration in early care and education: What can and should we expect? *Young Children* 47 (1): 51–56.

Leister, C. 1993. Working with parents of different cultures. *Dimensions of Early Childhood* 21 (2): 6–9.

Lowenthal, B. 1992. Collaborative training in the education of early childhood educators. *Teaching Exceptional Children* 24 (4): 25–29.

Lubeck, S. 1994. The politics of developmentally appropriate practice: Exploring issues of culture, class, and curriculum. In *Diversity and developmentally appropriate practices,* eds. B.L. Mallory & R.S. New, 17–43. New York: Teachers College Press.

Mahoney, G., C. Robinson, & A. Powell. 1992. Focusing on parent-child interaction: The bridge to developmentally appropriate practices. *Topics in Early Childhood Special Education* 12 (1): 105–20.

Mallory, B.L. 1994. Inclusive policy, practice, and theory for young children with developmental differences. In *Diversity and developmentally appropriate practices,* eds. B.L. Mallory & R.S. New, 44–61. New York: Teachers College Press.

Morgan, J.L., E.C. Guetzloe, & W. Swan. 1991. Leadership for local interagency coordinating councils. *Journal of Early Intervention* 15 (3): 255–67.

Ross, H.W. 1992. Integrating infants with disabilities? Can "ordinary" caregivers do it? *Young Children* 47 (3): 65–71.

Salisbury, C.L. 1991. Mainstreaming during the early childhood years. *Exceptional Children* 58: 146–55.

Swan, W.W., & J.L. Morgan. 1993. *Collaborating for comprehensive services for young children and their families: The local interagency coordinating council.* Baltimore: Paul H. Brookes.

Templeman, T.P., H.D. Fredericks, & T. Udell. 1989. Integration of children with moderate and severe handicaps into a day care center. *Journal of Early Intervention* 13 (4): 315–28.

Thorp, E.K., & J.A. McCollum. 1988. Defining the infancy specialization in early childhood special education. In *Early childhood special education: Birth to three,* eds. J.B. Jordan, J.J. Gallagher, P.L. Hutinger, & M.B. Karnes, 147–62. Reston, VA: Council for Exceptional Children.

Wakefield, A.P. 1993. Developmentally appropriate practice: "Figuring things out." *The Educational Forum* 57: 134–43.

SECTION 3. NBPTS STANDARDS FOR EARLY CHILDHOOD/GENERALIST CERTIFICATION

RECOMMENDATIONS OF THE NATIONAL BOARD FOR PROFESSIONAL TEACHING STANDARDS

OVERVIEW

The world-class schools America requires cannot exist without a world-class teaching force; the two go hand in hand. Many excellent teachers already work in the nation's schools, but their work is often unrewarded and underappreciated, their knowledge and skills unacknowledged and underutilized. Delineating outstanding practice and recognizing those who achieve it are important first steps in shaping the kind of teaching profession America needs. This is the core challenge embraced by the National Board for Professional Teaching Standards (NBPTS). Founded in 1987 with a broad base of support from governors, teacher union and school board leaders, administrators, college and university officials, business executives, foundations, and concerned citizens, NBPTS is a nonprofit, nonpartisan organization governed by a 63-member Board of Directors, the majority of whom are teachers. Committed to basic reform in American education, the National Board recognizes that teaching is at the heart of education and, further, that the single most important action the nation can take to improve schools is to strengthen teaching. To this end, the National Board has embarked on a three-part mission:

- to establish high and rigorous standards for what accomplished teachers should know and be able to do;

- to develop and operate a national voluntary system to assess and certify teachers who meet these standards; and

- to advance related education reforms for the purpose of improving student learning in American schools.

Achieving this mission will elevate the teaching profession, educate the public about the demands and complexity of excellent practice, and increase our chances of attracting and retaining in the profession talented college graduates with many other promising career options.

National Board Certification is more than a system for recognizing and rewarding accomplished teachers, however. It represents both an opportunity to rethink the way the profession organizes itself for the continuing growth and development of its members and a chance to design new ways to organize and manage schools to capitalize on the expertise of accomplished teachers. Together with other reforms, certification can be a catalyst for significant change in the profession and in American education.

The Philosophical Context

The standards presented here lay the foundation for the Early Childhood/Generalist certificate. They represent a professional consensus on the critical aspects of practice that distinguish exemplary teachers in this field from novice or journeymen teachers. Cast in terms of actions that teachers take to advance student outcomes, these standards also incorporate the essential knowledge, skills, dispositions and commitments that allow teachers to practice at a high level. Like all National Board standards, they rest on a fundamental philosophical foundation, expressed in the NBPTS policy statement *What Teachers Should Know and Be Able to Do.* That statement identifies five core propositions:

1. TEACHERS ARE COMMITTED TO STUDENTS AND THEIR LEARNING

National Board Certified Teachers are dedicated to making knowledge accessible to all students. They act on the belief that all students can learn. They treat students equitably, recognizing the individual differences that distinguish their students, one from the other, and taking account of these differences in their practice. They adjust their practice, as appropriate, based on observation and knowledge of their students' interests, abilities, skills, knowledge, family circumstances, and peer relationships.

Accomplished teachers understand how students develop and learn. They incorporate the prevailing theories of cognition and intelligence in their practice. They are aware of the influence of context and culture on behavior. They develop students' cognitive capacity and their respect for learning. Equally important, they foster students' self-esteem, motivation, character, civic responsibility, and their respect for individual, cultural, religious, and racial differences.

2. TEACHERS KNOW THE SUBJECTS THEY TEACH AND HOW TO TEACH THOSE SUBJECTS TO STUDENTS

National Board Certified Teachers have a rich understanding of the subject(s) they teach and appreciate how knowledge in their subject is created, organized, linked to other disciplines, and applied to real-world settings. While faithfully representing the collective wisdom of our culture and upholding the value of disciplinary knowledge, they also develop the critical and analytical capacities of their students.

Accomplished teachers command specialized knowledge of how to convey and reveal subject matter to students. They are aware of the preconceptions and background knowledge that students typically bring to each subject and of strategies and instructional materials that can be of assistance. They understand where difficulties are likely to arise and modify their practice accordingly. Their instructional repertoire allows them to create multiple paths to the subjects they teach, and they are adept at teaching students how to pose and solve their own problems.

3. TEACHERS ARE RESPONSIBLE FOR MANAGING AND MONITORING STUDENT LEARNING

National Board Certified Teachers create, enrich, maintain, and alter instructional settings to capture and sustain the interest of their students and to make the most effective use of time. They are also adept at engaging students and adults to assist their teaching and at enlisting their colleagues' knowledge and expertise to complement their own.

Accomplished teachers command a range of generic instructional techniques, know when each is appropriate, and can implement them as needed. They are as aware of ineffectual or damaging practice as they are devoted to elegant practice.

They know how to engage groups of students to ensure a disciplined learning environment and how to organize instruction to allow the school's goals for students to be met. They are adept at setting norms for social interaction among students and between students and teachers. They understand how to motivate students to learn and how to maintain their interest even in the face of temporary failure.

National Board Certified Teachers can assess the progress of individual students as well as that of the class as a whole. They employ multiple methods for measuring student growth and understanding and can clearly explain student performance to parents.

4. TEACHERS THINK SYSTEMATICALLY ABOUT THEIR PRACTICE AND LEARN FROM EXPERIENCE

National Board Certified Teachers are models of educated persons, exemplifying the virtues they seek to inspire in students—curiosity, tolerance, honesty, fairness, respect for diversity, and appreciation of cultural differences—and the capacities that are prerequisites for intellectual growth: the ability to reason and take multiple perspectives, to be creative and take risks, and to adopt an experimental and problem-solving orientation.

Accomplished teachers draw on their knowledge of human development, subject matter and instruction, and their understanding of their students to make principled judgments about sound practice. Their decisions are not only grounded in the literature but also in their experience. They engage in lifelong learning, which they seek to encourage in their students.

Striving to strengthen their teaching, National Board Certified Teachers critically examine their practice, seek to expand their repertoire, deepen their knowledge, sharpen their judgment and adapt their teaching to new findings, ideas, and theories.

5. TEACHERS ARE MEMBERS OF LEARNING COMMUNITIES

National Board Certified Teachers contribute to the effectiveness of the school by working collaboratively with other professionals on instructional policy, curriculum development, and staff development. They can evaluate school progress and the allocation of school resources in light of their understanding of state and local educational objectives. They are knowledgeable about specialized school and community resources that can be engaged for their students' benefit and are skilled at employing such resources as needed.

Accomplished teachers find ways to work collaboratively and creatively with parents, engaging them productively in the work of the school.

The Certification Framework

Using these five core principles as a springboard, NBPTS sets standards and awards certificates in more than 30 fields. Most of these fields are defined by two dimensions: the developmental level of the students and the subject or subjects being taught. The first dimension embraces four overlapping student development levels:

- Early Childhood, ages 3–8
- Middle Childhood, ages 7–12
- Early Adolescence, ages 11–15
- Adolescence and Young Adulthood, ages 1–18+

The second dimension highlights the substantive focus of a teacher's practice, allowing most teachers to select either a subject-specific or a generalist certificate. At the Early Adolescence level, for example, teachers are able to pursue either a generalist certificate or a certificate in English language arts, mathematics, science, or social studies-history. Teachers seeking certification at the Middle Childhood level have a similar choice. The framework of certificates also includes a generalist certificate at the Early Childhood level and subject-specific certificates at the Adolescence and Young Adulthood levels. In some fields, developmental levels are joined together (for example, Early Adolescence through Young Adulthood/Vocational Education) to recognize the commonalities that hold practice together at those levels.

A third dimension comes into play in two other areas: the special knowledge associated with teaching children with exceptional needs, in the first instance, and the special knowledge associated with teaching those for whom English is a new language, in the second.

Standards and Assessment Development

Standards committees are appointed for each of the various certificate fields. The committees are generally made up of 15 members who are broadly representative of exemplary professionals in their field and a majority of whom are teachers regularly engaged in practice with students in the field in question. Other members are typically experts in child development, teacher education, and the relevant discipline(s). The standards committees recommend to the National Board the specific standards for each field, which are then disseminated widely for public critique and comment and subsequently revised as necessary.

Determining whether candidates meet the standards requires performance-based assessment methods that are fair, valid, and reliable and that call on teachers to demonstrate principled, professional judgments in a variety of situations. Assessment Development Laboratories (ADLs), working with standards committee members, develop assessment exercises and pilot test them with small groups of teachers. The ADLs are selected through a process of open competition and merit review and are composed of a mix of education measurement experts and educators with deep roots in the certification field. The assessment process that has emerged from the first ADLs is structured around two key activities: (1) the compilation of a teacher's portfolio of practice during the course of a school year and (2) participation in one or two days of assessment center activities during the summer.

Teachers prepare their portfolios by gathering student learning products and other teaching artifacts and providing analyses of their practice. At the assessment center, teachers take part in exercises that are organized around challenging issues that teachers in their field face on a regular basis. The portfolio is designed to capture teaching in real-time, real-life settings, thus allowing NBPTS to examine how teachers translate knowledge and theory into practice. It also yields the most valued evidence NBPTS collects—videos of practice and samples of student work. The videos and student work are accompanied by commentaries on the goals and purposes of instruction, the effectiveness of the practice, teachers' reflections on what occurred, and their rationales for the professional judgments they have made. In addition, the portfolio allows candidates to document their accomplishments in contributing to the advancement of the profession and the improvement of schooling (be it at the local, state, or national level), and to document their ability to work constructively with their students' families.

Teachers report that the portfolio is a professional development vehicle of considerable power, in part because it challenges the historic isolation of teachers from their peers. It accomplishes this, in the first instance, by actively encouraging candidates to seek the advice and counsel of their professional colleagues, be they across the hall or across the country, as candidates build their portfolios. It also requires teachers in the healthiest of ways to critically examine the underlying assumptions of their practice and the results of their efforts. This emphasis on reflection is highly valued by teachers who go through the process, as it stands in sharp contrast to the norms of their professional lives in which such systematic inquiry is rarely encouraged.

The assessment center exercises are designed to complement the portfolio, validate that the knowledge and skills exhibited in the portfolio are, in fact, accurate reflections of what candidates know and can do, and give candidates an opportunity to demonstrate knowledge and skills not sampled in the portfolio due to the candidate's specific teaching assignment. For example, high school science teachers assigned to teach only physics in a given year might be hard-pressed to demonstrate in their portfolio broad knowledge of biology. Given that NBPTS standards for science teachers place high value on such capabilities, another strategy for data collection is necessary. The assessment center exercises are designed to fill this gap and otherwise augment the portfolio. The exercises sample the breadth of the content knowledge and pedagogy associated with the certificate field through authentic scenarios that allow candidates to confront important instructional matters even as they are removed from the immediacy of the classroom. Each candidate's work is examined by assessors who are themselves highly accomplished teachers in the certificate field.

NBPTS adopted this model of teacher assessment, in part, because traditional teacher tests enjoy little legitimacy in the eyes of teachers and because their validity in gauging the complexities of exemplary practice is suspect by the psychometric community as well. NBPTS believes that a valid assessment of accomplished practice must allow for the variety of forms sound practice takes, must sample from the range of ways of knowing required for teaching, and must place assessments of teaching knowledge and skill in appropriate contexts. Teaching is not just about knowing things; it is about the use of knowledge—knowledge of learners and learning, of schools and subjects—in the service of helping students grow and develop. Consequently, NBPTS believes that the most valid teacher assessment processes are those that engage candidates in the activities of teaching activities that require the display and use of teaching knowledge and skill and that allow teachers the opportunity to explain and justify their actions.

In addition, in its assessment development work, NBPTS expects to explore and, where appropriate, use state-of-the-art technology for assessment; ensure broad representation of the diversity that exists within the profession in all stages of the development process; engage the pertinent disciplinary and specialty associations at key points in the process; work in close collaboration with appropriate state agencies, academic institutions, and independent research and education organizations; establish procedures to detect and eliminate instances of external and internal bias with respect to age, gender, and racial and ethnic background of teacher candidates; select the method exhibiting the least adverse impact when given a choice among equally valid assessments; and have the certification process provide both information that will assist teachers in preparing for the assessment and constructive feedback, especially for those candidates who do not at first meet NBPTS standards.

Once a certificate has been thoroughly tested and found to meet the National Board's requirements for validity, reliability, and fairness, eligible teachers may apply for National Board Certification. To be eligible, a teacher must hold a baccalaureate degree from an accredited institution; have a minimum of three years of teaching experience at the early childhood, elementary, middle or high school level; and, where it is required, hold a state teaching license. Those who choose to participate in this year-long process usually come away stronger for the effort.

Strengthening Teaching and Improving Learning

A system of National Board Certification that commands the respect of the profession and the public can make a critical difference in how communities and policymakers view teachers, how teachers view themselves, and how teachers improve their practice throughout their careers. National Board Certification has the potential to yield such significant results for American education, in part, because it marks the first attempt to forge a national professional consensus on the critical aspects of accomplished practice in each teaching field. The traditional conversation about teacher competence has focused on beginning teachers. Yet, unless we believe that the professional development of teachers should conclude the day novice teachers are hired, this new conversation about accomplished practice is essential.

Developing standards of accomplished practice has the potential to lift the entire profession as the standards make public the knowledge, skills, and dispositions that set accomplished teachers apart from journeymen. However, converting such standards into a system for the advanced certification of teachers promises much more. A mechanism that can identify accomplished teachers in a fair and trustworthy manner can accelerate efforts to build school organizations, structures and career paths that look significantly different from the flat, undifferentiated approach that typically gives novice teachers much more responsibility than they can sensibly handle; fails to take best advantage of the knowledge, wisdom, and expertise of accomplished teachers; and encourages many exemplary practitioners to leave the classroom for greater status, authority, and compensation.

By holding accomplished teachers to high and rigorous standards, National Board Certification has the potential to leverage change along several key fronts, for example:

- changing what it means to have a career in teaching by breaking the impasse between labor and management over recognizing and rewarding exemplary teachers and by making it possible for teachers to advance in responsibility, status, and compensation without having to leave the classroom;

- changing the culture of teaching by accelerating growth in the knowledge base of teaching, by placing real value on professional judgment and elegant practice in all its various manifestations, and by encouraging among teachers the search for new knowledge and better practice through a steady regimen of collaboration and reflection with peers and others;

- changing the way schools are organized and managed by creating a vehicle that facilitates the establishment of lead teacher positions and thus provides accomplished teachers with greater authority and autonomy in the making of instructional decisions and greater responsibility for sharing their expertise to strengthen the practice of others;

- changing the nature of teacher preparation and ongoing professional development by laying a standards-based foundation for a fully articulated career development path that begins with prospective teachers and continues with novice, journeymen, and, ultimately, highly accomplished teachers; and

- changing the way school districts think about hiring and compensating teachers by encouraging administrators and school boards to search for highly accomplished teachers, rather than the those who can be hired at the lowest salary, and to reward excellence in teaching.

While National Board Certification has been designed with the entire country in mind, each state and locality will decide for itself how best to encourage teachers to stand for advanced certification and how best to take advantage of the expertise of the National Board Certified Teachers in their midst. An early example of state action in support of National Board Certification comes from North Carolina, where legislation has been enacted that provides funds to pay the certification fee for teachers who complete the process. This legislation also funds release time for candidates to work on their portfolios and prepare for the assessment center exercises and provides a 4% salary increase for teachers who achieve National Board Certification. Other states have adopted or are in the process of adopting legislative initiatives that acknowledge National Board Certification and offer incentives for certification. At the local level, to give just two examples, school districts in Boston, Massachusetts, and Rochester, New York, have agreed to absorb the fee for the assessment process and give National Board Certified Teachers special consideration for "lead teacher" assignments.

As this growing support at the state and local level suggests, National Board Certification is being recognized for the rich professional development experience it has proven to be. In addition, as it provides states and localities a lever to more sensibly structure teachers' roles and responsibilities and to better organize schools to take advantage of the wisdom of our strongest teachers, National Board Certification can act in concert with other initiatives to dramatically improve education for America's youth.

Introduction to Early Childhood/ Generalist Standards

Early childhood teachers have the unique opportunity to introduce young children to the challenges and rewards of learning in classroom settings. Each year, teachers in Head Start centers, child care agencies, and a variety of prekindergarten programs welcome 3- and 4-year-old children to the formal community of learners. Other early childhood professionals open the doors of kindergarten and primary-grade classrooms and provide students with their first elementary school experiences. It is their rewarding task to usher the child from the private world of home and family to the more public world of formal education. They relish their roles as the orchestrator of a cohesive community of young learners and take pride in their abilities to create an environment where children with often vastly differing backgrounds, abilities, and needs work together successfully. These teachers work to help children gain the knowledge, skills, habits, and dispositions toward learning that will be crucial for their later success in school and life.

Accomplished early childhood teachers enjoy and appreciate young children. They love their unbridled enthusiasm and curiosity and the excitement that they bring to their explorations and to the new things they are learning every day. They are engaged by the variety and diversity of their charges across many dimensions, including their talents, interests, and cultures. They welcome the challenge and responsibility of guiding young children through their ever-expanding and dynamic worlds. They apply what they know about how children grow and develop to create activities that allow young people to use both the resources around them and their own abilities as pathways to learning. These teachers relish children's experiments with language, sounds, and images as they build their expressive repertoire. They enjoy watching children expand their worlds to include new friends and experiences and a whole range of never-before-experienced emotions and feelings, from the pride at being able to demonstrate a unique skill to the wonder and surprise at exploring a found bird's nest or complex pattern in a picture. They are aware that children do not come to them as empty vessels, all having begun making sense of the world long before they arrive at school. Their primary goal is to help children understand themselves and the world around them while they develop the skills and knowledge essential for thinking and problem solving and expanding their sense of confidence in their abilities.

As generalists, early childhood teachers develop skills and knowledge across all areas of the curriculum. To do so they draw on a wide range of subject matter knowledge and pedagogy. This allows them to meet the needs of young children who grow and develop sporadically and to respond effectively to groups of students who may be of the same age but at vastly different points in their development. Whether teaching 3-year-olds in a child development center or 8-year-olds in third grade, they advance student understanding and respond to the capacity and interests of their students.

Today's early childhood teachers work with a rich melange of eager learners from a wide range of backgrounds and with a variety of experiences and personal challenges. They teach young children who are maturing and developing skills and acquiring knowledge at different rates and more typically in "fits and starts" rather than in a smoothly incremental fashion. Successful early childhood teachers are distinguished by their skill at recognizing and responding to the individual differences children bring to the classroom. This takes several forms, including the following:

- Creating curriculum to build on children's present knowledge and understandings and move them to more sophisticated and in-depth skills, knowledge, concepts, and performances. Exemplary teachers calibrate their responses to their students, designing activities to the child's "proximal zone" for learning and development.

- Employing a range of instructional strategies and resources to match the variety of students and to provide each student several ways to explore important ideas, skills, and concepts. They understand how to work as facilitators, coaches, models, evaluators, managers, and advocates. They know how to utilize various forms of play, different strategies for grouping students, and different types of media and materials.

- Observing and assessing young children in the context of ongoing classroom life. They are skilled in collecting and interpreting a variety of types of evidence to evaluate where each child is in a sequence or continuum of learning and development. They know how to move from assessment to decisions about curriculum, social support, and teaching strategies to increase the prospects for successful learning.

- Understanding and respecting the diverse cultures, values, languages, and family backgrounds of their students, using community people and settings as resources for learning, and involving parents and families as active partners in the child's total development.

Like the conductor of a great orchestra, teachers make and execute dozens of complex decisions as they create the symphony that is their work with children. Each moment presents the opportunity for them to respond creatively to the unique challenges of classroom life. They are highly sophisticated analysts who apply observations of individual children and of the overall environment to guide their judgments and responses. They reflect on their own performances—considering student progress, seeking the views of colleagues and parents, and thinking about trends and options and the consequences of their choices.

While seeing to the needs of individuals, exemplary teachers must also be responsible to the group. It is an accomplished art to attend to the needs of each child while also managing a sizeable and active group enterprise. Accomplished teachers make children feel "special" in the midst of a crowd, allowing them to experience the pleasure of being one of the group, while at the same time they make the crowd an enjoyable, harmonious place to be.

Historically, the important work and achievements of early childhood teachers have gone unnoticed and have been underappreciated. The misconception was that young children were easier to teach than other students and did not need the strongest teachers. Attitudes are shifting. More and more, society is appreciating the complexity and significance of learning during the early childhood period. More resources are coming to preschool, child care, kindergarten, and primary-grade programs, and more healthy scrutiny is coming to the quality of the environments and those who work there. Today, there is a growing recognition that high-quality early childhood teaching is critical to our society's future. These standards are presented, in part, to foster and accelerate this progress in the profession of early childhood teaching.

The Standards Format

One of the essential tensions in translating the National Board's five propositions of accomplished practice into standards concerns the difference between the "analysis of " and the "practice of " teaching. The analysis of teaching tends to fragment the profession into any number of discrete duties, such as designing learning activities, managing the classroom, and monitoring student progress. Teaching as it actually occurs, on the other hand, is a seamless activity. Everything the accomplished teacher knows through study, research, and experience is brought to bear daily in the classroom in the form of literally dozens of decisions that shape the learning environment. These judgments range from the tactical to the strategic, frequently require balancing the competing claims of several important instructional goals, draw on observations of particular students and settings, and are subject to revision based on continuing developments in the classroom. In the real world such functions as planning learning activities, motivating effort, assessing progress, or maintaining classroom discipline do not happen in isolation. Rather, they are skillfully interwoven strands in the single, sturdy fabric of excellent practice.

The paradox, then, is that any attempt to write standards that "take apart" what accomplished teachers know and are able to do, to a certain extent, also will distort the holistic nature of how teaching actually takes place. That much having been said, however, the fact remains: there are certain identifiable commonalities that characterize the many styles of accomplished practice in teaching young children. These "big ideas" are the focus here. They have been set out in the form of eight standards, the description of which makes up the heart of this section.

It should be acknowledged at the outset that these specific standards are not the only way the task of describing accomplished early childhood teaching could have been approached. Nor is each standard of equal weight. No linearity, atomization, or hierarchy in this vision of excellent teaching is implied. Instead, the standards are presented as aspects of early childhood teaching that are analytically separable for the purposes of this writing but which are not discrete when they operate in real time.

The format follows a two-fold approach to describe the eight standards:

1. **Summary of the standard** is a succinct statement of one aspect of the practice of accomplished Early Childhood/Generalist teachers. Each of the standards is couched in terms of observable teacher actions that have an impact on students.

2. **Elaboration** provides texture for the standard along with an explanation of what teachers need to know and value if they are to satisfy the standard at a high level. This includes descriptions of their orientation to children, their distinctive roles and responsibilities, and their stance toward a range of ethical and intellectual challenges that regularly confront them.

The Standards in Summary

The requirements for National Board Certification as an Early Childhood/Generalist are organized around the following eight standards. These standards have been ordered as they have to facilitate understanding, not to assign priorities. They are each important facets of the art and science of teaching young children. In fact, in the course of excellent early childhood teaching, teachers often demonstrate several of these standards concurrently as they skillfully weave their knowledge, skills, and dispositions into a rich tapestry of exemplary practice.

I. UNDERSTANDING YOUNG CHILDREN

Teachers use their knowledge of child development and their relationships with children and families to understand children as individuals and to plan in response to their unique needs and potentials.

II. PROMOTING CHILD DEVELOPMENT AND LEARNING

Teachers promote children's physical, emotional, linguistic, creative, intellectual, social, and cognitive development by organizing the environment in ways that best facilitate the development and learning of young children.

III. KNOWLEDGE OF INTEGRATED CURRICULUM

Based on their knowledge of academic subjects and how young children learn, teachers design and implement developmentally appropriate learning experiences within and across the disciplines.

IV. MULTIPLE TEACHING STRATEGIES FOR MEANINGFUL LEARNING

Teachers use a variety of methods and materials to promote individual development, meaningful learning, and social cooperation.

V. ASSESSMENT

Teachers know the strengths and weaknesses of various assessment methodologies, continually monitor children's activities and behavior, and analyze this information to improve their work with children and parents.

VI. REFLECTIVE PRACTICE

Teachers regularly analyze, evaluate, and strengthen the quality and effectiveness of their work.

VII. FAMILY PARTNERSHIPS

Teachers work with and through parents and families to support children's learning and development.

VIII. PROFESSIONAL PARTNERSHIPS

Teachers work with colleagues to improve programs and practices for young children and their families.

Standard I: Understanding Young Children

TEACHERS USE THEIR KNOWLEDGE OF CHILD DEVELOPMENT AND THEIR RELATIONSHIPS WITH CHILDREN AND FAMILIES TO UNDERSTAND CHILDREN AS INDIVIDUALS AND TO PLAN IN RESPONSE TO THEIR UNIQUE NEEDS AND POTENTIALS.

Accomplished early childhood teachers know how young children develop and learn; know the culture, history, and values of the communities and families they serve; and know the attributes of the individual children in their care. Their knowledge of young children in general and the children in their own class in particular continues to grow as they spend time observing and learning from children. This knowledge serves them in many ways, including planning their overall program and schedule in a fashion that will engage children's interests, evaluating and creating materials and resources, and providing a context for assessing children's progress. Most of all, their knowledge of young children helps them interpret and understand the actions and responses of their students and fosters an appreciative stance toward them as unique individuals.

Teachers Know How Young Children Grow and Develop

Teachers[1] keep up-to-date in their knowledge of early childhood development, including advancements in cognitive science. They know that all children arrive at their first formal schooling as seasoned learners and explorers with a wide range of past experiences, some of which may have been positive and others that may have been negative. They understand that young children vary considerably, one from another, in the pattern and pace of their growth, thinking, language, and social capacities due to individual differences, influences of home culture and language, and special learning and developmental problems. They recognize when a child's pattern of growth or development varies significantly from what might be expected—such as when an unusual skill or ability is manifest or when there is a noticeably atypical struggle acquiring a skill. They note such variations and see to it that the child has access to additional support.

Teachers understand the patterns of physical development in young children and the links between physical health and successful experience in early childhood classrooms. They know that promoting increasing skill, independence, and confidence in using large and small muscles, in physical coordination, and in using different senses for learning is a vital aspect of early childhood classrooms and programs. For example, you would notice in the daily schedule of such teachers ample time allotted for children to engage in physical activity. While working on a skill in mathematics, the children might be singing or clapping their hands, sorting through a bag of beads, or doing a variety of activities that afford them multiple ways to grasp important mathematical ideas.

Teachers understand that children develop cognitive abilities in different ways and at different rates. Some children learn better when they have a chance to move. Others respond to music or when creating their own

---

1. All references to teachers in this section, whether stated explicitly or not, refer to accomplished Early Childhood/Generalist teachers. The examples that appear are intended to provide a modest sampling of the ways in which accomplished teachers meet the needs of children across the development range for this certificate. Many pertain to accomplished practice for only a portion of this span.

works of art. Teachers know that young children build understanding from concrete experiences, that children learn simple concepts and then use these concepts to understand more complex ideas. Interacting with materials and other people gives children the opportunity to interpret their experience in order to make sense of the world. These teachers also recognize the importance of imagination in the development of young children. Through their imaginative lives, children gain a better understanding of the world and their place in it, and thus gain confidence in their ability to function securely and with a sense of control. Creative expression and play help to nurture children's imaginative lives and help them organize their thinking and make sense out of otherwise chaotic or confusing events. Therefore, these teachers provide multiple opportunities for children to extend their imaginations through play, free exploration, creative dramatics, and in other ways that are child centered.

Teachers understand that children's success on academic tasks depends on their willingness to try new tasks, to put forth persistent effort, and to believe that they can perform at high levels. And, just as self-esteem contributes to academic performance, the reverse is also true. Children who work well in classrooms and experience tangible success view themselves as more competent and valuable. Teaching children to cooperate with adults and peers and to carry out classroom routines is also an important agenda in the early primary grades. Therefore, exemplary early childhood practitioners know how young children develop social and intellectual capacities and use that knowledge to establish the classroom environment and routines and, most importantly, to govern their personal interactions with children.

Teachers' understanding of learning is shaped by language, culture, family, and community values as well as individual attributes and talent. They are aware of cultural differences in social conventions, authority structures, and age-related expectations. They know that children's self-esteem and personal identity evolve from their place in their family and culture. They know that children are alert for cues that teachers respect, understand, and value them for the knowledge and social competence they have developed. Teachers therefore adapt their program in ways that attempt to ensure that all children will have success in achieving the large academic and social goals they have set out for them. They also hold as an important outcome the development of bridges from the life of the home to the life of the school and the larger community.

TEACHERS RECOGNIZE AND CAPITALIZE ON THE DIVERSITY AND COMMONALITY THAT EXIST AMONG THEIR STUDENTS

Early childhood teachers view student diversity, including the physical and intellectual variability of children, as an opportunity for a richer social and learning environment. To be successful in acting on this belief, teachers need to be articulate about their own culture, show curiosity about other people's history and beliefs, and be aware of their own responses to diversity. Such teachers are active in investigating the culture and history of their students and the school's community (see also "Standard VII—Family Partnerships"). They seek out people, experiences, and other resources that will help them understand the strengths, accomplishments, and mores of children's families and neighborhoods and the history and values that form the context for how their students grow up. They show respect for each child's own background, and they seek to introduce children to the range of other cultures in the community and in the larger society and to help them begin to recognize both what they hold in common with children in other settings as well as what distinguishes them from their counterparts. They know how to build connections among children's families, cultures, communities, and student work. They recognize and make use of the ways that children from different cultures may have of understanding their world and use such understandings as a bridge to further learning. Knowing that children who are from families that have recently arrived in the United States may have their own unique repertoire of songs, games, and stories, these teachers find ways to encourage such children to share their cultures and enrich the learning for all.

Teachers also understand that student diversity can create tensions among children. In addition, teachers' own values and style of speaking and interacting and the public purposes of schooling may be in conflict with their students' family culture. For example, teachers seek to foster children's abilities to make individual choices and think independently. In some communities, most decisions are made by elders or by group consensus, and the valued attribute for children is conformity. Parents in such communities may respond to children's efforts to express themselves and make choices, perceiving these as threats to adult authority in the home. Teachers recognize these concerns and address them through discussions with parents, peers, and community members, without either relinquishing their important goals or being disrespectful to parents or community members. They honor their professional responsibilities and call upon school district and professional guidelines and standards to inform their decision making.

At the same time, teachers recognize that children from all backgrounds and communities may share many of the same interests, have similar successes and challenges, and are excited by many of the same kinds of experiences and learning opportunities. They know, for example, that most children will respond enthusiastically to being read an exciting story or to having the chance to prepare a simple dish and share it with their friends. So while they capitalize on the diversity among their classroom population as an opportunity for learning, they also build upon their commonalities as a tool for promoting classroom cohesiveness and for fostering attitudes conducive to participating in democratic institutions.

While attending to the overall management of the classroom, teachers seek to maximize opportunities to engage each child, building a cumulative picture of children's strengths and interests, how they speak, reason, and interact socially. As described in "Standard V—Assessment," they continually observe and listen to children, not principally to compare their performance to peers or grade-level objectives but rather to understand them as individuals and to inform practice. Teachers talk with the children in their classroom to learn about their ideas, values, concerns, and hopes. They use this information in presenting subjects, posing challenges, and interpreting students' responses. Teachers also recognize that there may be a healthy and necessary tension among the goals of accommodating student choice and interest, establishing a workable and coherent structure to their programs, and mediating for specific special needs that may be present in their population. Consequently, they seek to steer a middle course, choosing a route that makes sense for their students and communities.

STANDARD II: PROMOTING CHILD DEVELOPMENT AND LEARNING

TEACHERS PROMOTE CHILDREN'S PHYSICAL, EMOTIONAL, LINGUISTIC, CREATIVE, INTELLECTUAL, SOCIAL, AND COGNITIVE DEVELOPMENT BY ORGANIZING THE ENVIRNONMENT IN WAYS THAT BEST FACILITATE THE DEVELOPMENT AND LEARNING OF YOUNG CHILDREN.

Accomplished teachers use their knowledge of child development and learning to create a safe, caring, inclusive, and intellectually engaging environment to promote learning and all aspects of development. They carefully consider how to design and adjust the physical space (providing opportunities for movement and varied arrangements for group and individual activities), the social and emotional climate (an ambiance that encourages relationships that promote the participation of all students, safety and support for students taking intellectual risks), and the schedule, materials, and human resources of the classroom. The environment is responsive to the children's needs and capacities as they change over time. The teacher makes adjustments throughout the year, adding new materials and activities, adjusting the schedule, building on the interests and questions of the children, and involving them in decision making about group activities and problems. The teacher understands that the environment is a "second teacher," because young children learn by making choices and through their interaction with materials, peers, and adults.

TEACHERS UNDERSTAND THE CENTRAL ROLE OF PLAY IN CHILD DEVELOPMENT

Teachers understand the important role that the imaginative life of children plays in their development, and they know the ways in which play helps to promote development across all age levels. They therefore provide ample opportunities for various kinds of play within the school day. They encourage play because of the way it helps children develop thoughts, concepts, and communication. They understand the ways young children use play to express their ideas and feelings and to make their first attempts at symbolic representation. They also know how play can be an important vehicle for integrating and understanding content across the curriculum as well as for children to process other experiences they have had in their lives.

Teachers understand the process of play. They know that, as in any other activity, children need to "warm up." It often takes time for children to settle into productive play. They understand the ways that children move in and out of activities, leaving the group that is acting out a medical emergency when the restaurant group seems more appealing. They also know that children come in and out of role as they are playing, sometimes stopping mid-sentence to make a pronouncement in their "real" persona. They understand that some children have a hard time gaining access to a group because of their gender, because the other children are culturally different, or because they are shy or are still developing socially. Some children may think that certain types of activities are for boys and others are for girls, and still others have limited experience in any kind of play at all. Some children reach levels of exuberance that may not be appropriate to the space or may be potentially harmful to themselves or others. Teachers are attentive to such needs and work to help children gain access to play, manage play so that it stays within the boundaries of safety and sanity, and organize play so that it does not perpetuate or engender divisiveness or deteriorate into destructive, prejudicial, or other harmful behavior in their classrooms. One means of accomplishing this goal is to play alongside children, both to help enrich and extend play as well as to model for all the importance of the work they are doing when they are playing.

Teachers are also aware of the role of play in the development of character and how it can help children begin to deal with issues of justice and fairness. Conflict can occur in any play situation, and play also allows opportunities for children to practice generosity, fairness, tolerance, understanding, and other key character traits. Teachers, as they observe and play alongside their charges, take advantage of these opportunities to guide the development of character and to help children understand and manage their own responses when the game has not gone the way they wanted or when they perceive that an injustice has taken place.

Teachers know about and value the different forms of play, including indoor and outdoor play, solitary and group play, fantasy play, dramatic play, and directed and free play, and they create an environment that stimulates these different varieties and combinations. They also understand that play often presents opportunities for students to gain valuable knowledge, such as when children engage in a counting game or decide which building blocks make a construction more stable. Consequently, teachers provide a wide variety of materials and equipment for play and in the selection and use of all materials hold safety as a primary consideration. They understand the importance of providing non-representational materials, such as sand, water, blocks and other building materials, for open-ended play activities. They key into children's interest in particular topics or themes and locate materials that might lend themselves to role-playing activities.

Teachers are keen observers of children as they play, drawing inferences from children's behavior and dialogue during play situations. They understand the literal meaning of what they are watching and also are aware that very often children are using play metaphorically, to act out a range of emotions and ideas. They are aware of the social dynamics of the play group and, as they observe, may intervene strategically and appropriately to guide or to encourage the play or to get caught up in the spirit of fun. Their interventions may extend a concept from an earlier lesson, facilitate the social development of a member of the group, or solve a problem. They use their observations to gather further information about the children and to inform their design of class activities.

Teachers act as advocates of play. They can explain their allocation of time for games, outdoor play, and child-initiated forms of activity to parents, colleagues, and administrators. They are articulate and effective in discussing with parents and community leaders such issues as opportunities for play and recreation in community settings, the influence of television viewing on young children, the appropriate ages for children to engage in competitive team sports, and the provision for safe and well-equipped space for play outside of school and home.

TEACHERS FOSTER PHYSICAL HEALTH, DEVELOPMENT, AND GROWTH

Teachers understand the physical development and growth of young children. They create activities and a schedule that attends to the physical needs of young children for movement, rest, play, fine- and gross-motor development, health, and fitness. Teachers draw on a repertoire of movement activities from dance and physical education to give children a wide range of experience with movement. Children have daily opportunities for outdoor play and activities to develop physical skills and learn about their environment. They learn about health, nutrition, and safety through direct experience rather than admonitions, though teachers stand ready to warn children about activities and hazards in the immediate environment that might cause them harm. Younger children are provided with opportunities to develop daily living skills in eating, dressing, hygiene, and toileting. Teachers are alert to evidence of physical problems that may detract from a child's ability to learn (e.g., hearing or vision problems, illness, abuse, poor nutrition, dental problems, lack of sleep, indications of possible disabilities). They know that evidence of difficulty with certain kinds of movements may indicate a more serious problem. They work effectively with other staff, including nurses, physicians, special education staff, nutritionists, physical education teachers, dentists, coaches, and parents, to help develop appropriate intervention strategies for children with such problems. Physical development is not addressed solely through separate Physical Education and Health Education periods and specialized staff experts. Rather, the entire schedule and range of activities are designed to support health and physical development.

TEACHERS ENHANCE SOCIAL DEVELOPMENT AND SOCIAL SKILLS

Teachers understand the importance of social development in early childhood education and understand that the development of social skills and character are key to successful learning in groups and are core components of success for adults in work, family, civic, and community contexts. Also, they know that social interaction is critical to the child's linguistic and cognitive development. Teachers

know that children from ages 3 to 8 typically make tremendous progress in their level of skills in this area.

Accomplished teachers understand their responsibility for establishing a climate that fosters learning, setting norms for social interaction, and intervening to assist students in resolving disputes and conflicts. They help children develop social knowledge about learning in groups, behavioral expectations of peers and adults, and the need to adapt to classroom rules and routines as well as to the norms of society at large. This is the beginning of the early childhood social studies curriculum. Teachers also help to move children from primary concern about themselves to the ability to acknowledge the needs of others. They recognize that an important goal for many young children is to learn to exercise self-control, particularly in their interactions with other children and as they learn about being in public settings, such as in the classroom. They provide children with experiences and feedback that lead them to make choices that are appropriate in classroom settings and to learn to manage themselves in social situations. They view the development of character as an important goal and they model, recognize, and reward the virtues, such as honesty, fairness, and compassion. Whenever possible, they allow the children in their classrooms to participate in developing rules and guidelines for behavior and for settling their own disputes.

Teachers foster social responsibility by encouraging actions to support the common good and by helping students appreciate other points of view and balance a sense of self-worth with a recognition of dependence. Children have frequent opportunities to use skills, such as initiating and sustaining interactions, working collaboratively with others, planning, sharing, taking turns, negotiating differences, exhibiting tolerance, finding non-physical ways to resolve conflicts, and making decisions. These teachers appreciate the implications of instructional strategies for social relationships in the classroom. For instance, they group children in a variety of ways during the day, changing grouping patterns over time and regularly allowing children opportunities to choose their own groups or partners. They also provide opportunities for children to experience individual success, thereby fostering independence and a sense of personal accomplishment. Such skills can be enhanced in many settings, including multi-aged and non-graded groupings. Teachers use this variety of arrangements to allow children to learn to appreciate their different ways of learning and understanding.

Teachers work to build among children respect and appreciation for different cultures and races, genders, social classes and family types, and for other children whose backgrounds are different from their own. They do this, in part, through their grouping practices, by locating and creating instructional materials and learning experiences that are drawn from different cultures, and by, wherever possible, including the community in school events. In this same vein, they are adept at engaging family and community members as learning resources. They are also alert to stereotypes and deficit images in written materials, current events, and children's own play, language, and social interactions.

TEACHERS SUPPORT CHILDREN'S EMOTIONAL DEVELOPMENT AND SELF-RESPECT

Teachers work to enhance children's self-respect and confidence in learning in a variety of ways, seeking to promote independence, risk taking, and persistence in their students. In order to facilitate such growth, teachers establish relationships with their students to allow children to observe them closely and to better understand each child's

unique needs. They observe how their students feel about themselves, their work, and their place in the classroom community. They show respect for children by responding to their interests and concerns rather than only directing them. They balance the need to bring children into the social world with a respect for the privacy that each individual values. They use their understanding of child development to create activities that are challenging, attainable, and designed to foster children's natural desires to understand their environment and develop competence, for they know that as children recognize their growing competence in various spheres, reinforcement of their self-worth usually follows. They also select materials and activities that promote positive images of different races, genders, religions, and cultures and of individuals with physical or mental disabilities as one way to enhance the self-respect of all children.

Teachers serve as models in their enthusiasm for learning and commitment to hard work. They recognize their ability to encourage, support, and affirm children's work and their personal worth. But they also understand that self-respect develops as children gain autonomy from adults, through solving problems and coping with difficulties and setbacks. They also appreciate individuals differences in children's personality and temperament and in how children may acquire and show self-confidence.

Teachers are skilled at providing a blend of challenge and support in learning tasks and in their personal responses to each student. They are also skilled at dealing with stress and the consequences of violence in the lives of individuals and their communities. They know how to work with children who exhibit anger or a lack of social skills—perhaps taking a more nurturing approach or providing additional attention rather than labeling them as "emotionally disturbed." They also know when children need additional support to better manage their own behavior and are able to connect these children with the resources they need, recommending alternative services for children when it is appropriate and in the best interest of the child and of others in the class. These teachers know that very often children who have difficulty with their peers and with adults often lack the necessary social skills to be a part of a community. They therefore take on as an important part of their work the development in their students of both empathy for others and the skills to effectively join a group.

TEACHERS SUPPORT DEVELOPMENT OF CHILDREN'S LANGUAGE ACQUISITION

Teachers know that the acquisition of language skills is an essential developmental task of childhood. They understand the language acquisition process and know the stages children go through as they develop facility with language. They know that at this age many children are in transition from the language that is used at home to the more formal language of society. They help children understand that language is a powerful tool that allows them to organize and express their views and questions about the world and to communicate with other people. Teachers know that young children are at a particularly critical time in the acquisition and development of their language skills because of the special capacities they have at this age for language development. The activities and the environment that teachers create provide the children in their classrooms with a variety of opportunities to use oral and written language in order to carry out, understand, and give meaning to activities and relationships. Dialogue among children and between children and adults is treated as an especially important means to promote understanding. Exemplary teachers' knowledge of how children use language informs their efforts to enrich further

language development and helps them understand how students approach problems, their modes of understanding, and stages of conceptual development (see also "Standard III—Knowledge of Integrated Curriculum"). They take this tack, in part, out of a recognition that speaking, listening, reading, and writing are important means through which all subjects and activities are integrated.

The classrooms of such teachers are inclusive places where varieties of language are accepted and celebrated and where teachers can be found modeling a variety of uses and means of oral and written language. Many programs have children for whom English is a new language. Teachers are aware of the benefits and special challenges in helping children develop and maintain two or more languages and, to the best of their ability, encourage and promote literacy in these children's home language as they advance their ability to communicate in English. Simultaneously, they move children toward an understanding of the role of standard English in their future academic and economic success.

TEACHERS FACILITATE POSITIVE DISPOSITIONS AND APPROACHES TOWARD LEARNING

Teachers understand that every child comes to school with a vast amount of prior knowledge and experience and with a desire to continue learning. They know that children come to them with a wide range of ideas and misconceptions about the things they have been exposed to—in the media and in their communities—and that they have a curiosity and excitement about learning more. For example, teachers see their role as continuing to foster this excitement by introducing children to a wider range of resources and opportunities for learning. They know the importance of motivation in the learning process and use a variety of means to encourage children to do their best, being aware that, ultimately, self-direction and finding the pursuit of knowledge intrinsically valuable are important goals. Such teachers offer children opportunities to exhibit and enhance persistence, curiosity, willingness to take risks, and abilities to use peers and adults as resources.

They know that children exhibit these attributes in different ways and at different levels in different tasks, times, and situations. At the same time, teachers are keenly aware that not all children learn in the same way. For example, some children especially enjoy learning through auditory experiences. Others thrive through experiences that are tactile in nature. However, all children benefit from a variety of learning experiences that allow them to confront important ideas and concepts from several angles. Consequently, teachers create learning situations that maximize each child's unique approach to learning while also creating and maintaining an environment in which all participants feel safe to explore and discuss different approaches, responses, and understandings of tasks and activities. They also constantly observe what children do and listen to what they say to help figure out what support their students need to continue developing and learning.

Teachers value and model thinking and discourse about ideas as a worthwhile activity. They encourage children to explore phenomena, learn to solve problems in different ways, and share and test their explanations and interpretations with other students. Children need to feel they are respected as individuals; that it is natural and desirable for learners to differ in their ideas, opinions, and explanations; indeed, that many worthwhile questions do not have a single "right" answer. Given this level of uncertainty and potential for social and cognitive conflict, students need to feel safe to venture opinions, to make "mistakes," to understand that confusion is natural (even for adults), and to learn from the ideas of their peers. Accomplished teachers help children identify their questions and support their efforts to answer these questions.

Teachers understand the importance of creating a foundation for future learning during the early childhood years, not only in basic knowledge and skills but also in children's habits of mind and attitudes toward the subjects they will be learning. They give priority to helping children learn in a variety of ways: to understand concepts, to develop problem-solving and critical-thinking skills, to appreciate different responses to a question, and to relate information across the boundaries of traditional disciplines and between the classroom and community settings. For example, such teachers provide many opportunities for children to explore numerical concepts and problem-solving strategies through the use of manipulative materials and group discussions.

Teachers use their knowledge of child development and their observations about their own students to create challenging, meaningful, engaging learning experiences. They understand that children build knowledge and understanding on prior experiences and concepts. They are skilled at connecting children's interests and responses with longer-term curricular and developmental goals. They take the way that younger children learn into account in their teaching, using experience and hands-on material as the basis for developing concepts and understandings. For example, since every child is an "expert" in his or her neighborhood, work in science can begin with children observing, manipulating, and experimenting with materials around their homes and in school. Teachers also know that children have curiosity that ranges far beyond home and community and, through their exploration of books and other media, develop interests and curiosity about many complex ideas. Through experimentation, sampling, exploring, media, and other methods, they help students begin to make sense of a wide variety of ideas and phenomena.

STANDARD III: KNOWLEDGE OF INTEGRATED CURRICULUM

BASED ON THEIR KNOWLEDGE OF ACADEMIC SUBJECTS AND HOW YOUNG CHILDREN LEARN, TEACHERS DESIGN AND IMPLEMENT DEVELOPMENTALLY APPROPRIATE LEARNING EXPERIENCES WITHIN AND ACROSS THE DISCIPLINES.

Accomplished early childhood teaching involves the melding of knowledge, dispositions, and insights from child development with the structure of knowledge and concepts in the academic disciplines. Exemplary practice is neither exclusively child centered nor driven solely by curriculum content, but a rich and careful melding of both. Decisions about curriculum, activities, and materials are made for a variety of compelling reasons that include promoting worthwhile knowledge and concepts (categorized within the academic disciplines), developing skills that cut across the disciplines, helping youngsters apply such knowledge to issues that require a multidisciplinary approach, and making learning in schools personally relevant and captivating to students.

Early childhood teachers draw on their broad understanding of the core academic subjects (literacy and English language arts, mathematics, science, social studies, and the visual and performing arts) in planning and implementing integrative activities. They know the key concepts, ideas, and facts in each subject area that young children should understand and the typical ways children reason and talk about them; they know about the kinds of naive theories children develop about the world around them and the difficulties students are likely to encounter as they explore new terrain. They are also familiar with the different routes and stages of children's progress in developing skills, knowledge, dispositions, and understandings across these several dimensions.

Teachers working with children at the earliest ages often employ a considerable amount of cross-disciplinary teaching in their practice; in fact, in many of their classrooms an observer might be hard-pressed to identify the lines between a literature lesson, a science lesson, and an art project. Such teachers are adept at creating projects and experiences that foster the joining of skills and knowledge from multiple disciplines. They understand that many issues young children find fascinating do not fall easily into distinct disciplinary boxes nor do young children naturally think in terms of disciplines. Consequently, they orient their teaching based on what they know about how children construct knowledge. Those working with the oldest children at this developmental level may find themselves in departmentalized programs where such disciplinary distinctions may seem more apparent. Regardless of assignment or the way their instruction is organized, early childhood teachers have a strong grasp of the disciplinary knowledge that is the basis for their teaching. The disciplines inform the world of the teacher in supporting children's learning interests and needs.

Teachers use their knowledge of the disciplines to inform a variety of decisions and judgments: distinguishing between powerful, core ideas and topics and those of lesser importance; setting ambitious but reasonable expectations for student learning; and sequencing activities in ways that make sense conceptually. They work with other staff in planning curriculum and in judging the quality of materials and resources and to create themes and projects across subject areas that interest children and encourage them to develop and apply knowledge, skills, and ideas to real-world problems.

The following descriptions of the five subject-matter knowledge domains describe the major ideas, concepts, themes, and topics that early childhood generalists draw upon as they create learning experiences for their students.

THE ARTS

The arts—music, visual arts, performing arts, dance—are an integral part of the early childhood curriculum. Teachers have a broad background in the visual and performing arts that allows them to design activities and experiences that are appropriate and enriching for young children. They give students opportunities to create art, to look at and talk about art, and to develop an awareness of the arts in their everyday lives. They allow children to understand and experiment with various sources of inspiration for their work and to come up with their own ideas for expression and for understanding and using a variety of materials. Teachers know the kinds of tools, materials, and processes that are particularly useful and able to be manipulated by young children and help children learn to select, control, and experiment with a variety of media that help them facilitate their own expression. They expose children to a variety of art forms and help them to begin to identify their preferences and to discuss similarities and differences of various pieces. They help children understand that there are many different aesthetic approaches and responses to art and introduce the idea that while some viewers consider a particular work of art beautiful, others may find the same work unsettling or thought provoking. Using examples from a variety of cultures allows teachers to help expand children's understanding of different approaches to beauty and aesthetic expression. These teachers help children appreciate the forms of beauty in the world around them and to begin to manipulate their own aesthetic environments.

Young children are at a time in their physical development when coming to understand the functioning of their growing bodies is of particular importance, and many are able to acquire significant understanding of the world around them by the way they move through it. Dance and other forms of movement education are a particularly important part of the arts curriculum in that they allow teachers of young children to capitalize on their children's capacities and needs to move forward on a number of goals. These teachers have a repertoire of movement techniques and activities that they bring to their curriculum and provide time, place, and appropriate supervision to execute them.

Music is a central component of the lives of almost all children, and teachers make use of it in their teaching in a variety of ways. They introduce children to and help them appreciate different forms and styles of music, which in addition to helping children broaden their perceptions of the variety of music that abounds in the world also allows the teacher to enhance the study of other cultures and forms of expression. They begin to build in children a basic vocabulary for talking about music, introducing such concepts as rhythm, melody, and tone. They also provide opportunities for children to express themselves through music both through songs and through the playing of simple instruments, recognizing the way such performance enables forms of emotional expression that may not be available in others parts of children's lives. These teachers see music as a useful tool for extending other parts of the children's learning, when, for example, they use rhythm patterns to enhance a counting lesson or provide for unique word play in a way that only some songs can.

Recognizing that confidence building is an important aspect of artistic development, teachers provide activities that give children an opportunity to play as they practice a given artistic activity. Creative arts are used to express and understand knowledge and ideas in other disciplines (e.g., representational drawing and modeling in science or projects in literature or current events). Teachers promote children's knowledge of various criteria for evaluating the arts and enable students to begin to understand how the arts represent another way to perceive and interpret the world. Teachers show their own enjoyment and participation in the creative arts by creating, responding, questioning, and discussing various forms of the arts. They use artistic materials and experiences as another occasion for discussion and thinking about important and interesting questions and phenomena with students.

LITERACY AND ENGLISH LANGUAGE ARTS

Teachers are conversant in major theories, research, and controversies about teaching reading and writing. They create language arts programs that promote reading, writing, speaking, and listening skills and foster critical and creative thinking through the use of language. They draw on their knowledge of the key challenges and typical processes of initial development of these skills and capacities. They know how children learn language and how this process represents a model for teaching language arts. They also understand how children acquire a second language and can support learning by students whose first language is not English. They use this knowledge to design appropriate activities and experiences for children of different ages and to explain their teaching strategies to parents, administrators, and colleagues.

Teachers are aware of recent theory that provides insight into the nature of literacy. They understand that reading, writing, speaking, and listening are interrelated and mutually reinforcing. In particular, they know that literacy serves many purposes and that, therefore, children need to have a robust variety of experiences with reading, writing, and oral language. They also recognize that skilled reading involves integration of interacting systems of knowledge, including complex schemata such as story structure and more discrete knowledge such as letter recognition, and that readers use multiple cuing systems (e.g., letter shape, sentence context, story line) as they recognize words. They know that comprehension processes are guided by strategies whose development may be fostered among children of all ages through thoughtful discussion of books. Teachers also understand that reading builds on and extends oral language skills, including the ability to reflect on language, the development of a rich oral vocabulary, and the ability to communicate and understand complex thoughts through spoken language.

Recognizing the professional debates surrounding reading and language arts instruction, teachers strive to introduce children to the power of literacy and the joy of books while ensuring that all children acquire the requisite foundational knowledge and dispositions needed for reading success. Thus, they provide children the instruction they need to attend to and understand patterns of phoneme-grapheme correspondences, semantics and syntax, while also providing the richly varied range of experiences with spoken and written language necessary for literacy development.

Teachers create a rich environment for literacy learning, using language and stimulating stories that connect with what children already know and are curious about. In all classroom settings, including those where children's home languages are not English, teachers build upon the previous linguistic experience of their students, organizing their instruction in ways that take advantage of students' prior literacy experiences, and promote and encourage the ongoing development of language and literacy in English as well as in the language that is spoken in the home and community. They help children talk and write to express their ideas and feelings and to communicate with other people and read to clarify their ideas and learn from other people in their classroom, community, and the larger world. Such teachers create a variety of meaningful literacy activities that may include learning logs, diaries of solving problems in mathematics or science, conversations and discussions, various types of journals, correspondence with other people, and the use of signs, labels, charts, and lists in the classroom. They encourage play with words and sounds through such areas as rhymes, chants, and songs. They encourage a variety of forms of language and expression and show their own enjoyment and involvement in writing, literature, and conversation. This can be seen when exemplary teachers

- develop children's appreciation of literature and learning through books by regular exposure to different genres of children's literature, to literature from different cultures, and to good books of all sorts. They read regularly to the children in their class, and the children read to each other both to build enjoyment in reading and to model skills in comprehension and analysis. They encourage children to read on their own and provide them with multiple opportunities to do so.

- encourage children to discuss their thoughts and ideas about stories, the things they are learning in school, and their own experiences. Such metacognitive strategies are especially important for children who come from homes where the literary environment is modest or worse. They also provide opportunities for children to engage in critical and creative analysis of what they are reading.

- have children dictate individual and group stories, which are written and then read aloud so that they understand the connection between what is said and what is written. They then help children learn to begin to compose stories that have the conventions of written language as opposed to recorded speech.

- develop the process of writing, using oral language as the starting point, encouraging students to capture their ideas on paper in the form of drawings, scribbling, letters, and labels that eventually mature into more complete written text. Teachers understand the characteristics of emergent writing, which include invented spelling and lack of conventional mechanics. They know that invented spelling reflects children's efforts to communicate using print and is a powerful means for acquiring insight regarding children's linguistic growth. Therefore, they focus on responding to the nature of the content and ideas produced by their students. They know that children acquire skills at their own pace and are constantly monitoring skill development so as to assist in critical stages. As their children's experience as writers and readers grows, they are further able to develop in them an understanding of the importance of and proper use of conventions. Consequently, they do not ignore the conventions of grammar and spelling but provide such instruction as it becomes appropriate for each child. Children are encouraged to write and illustrate their own stories, poems, letters, books, and reports at progressive levels of skill and complexity. They write about experiences in and outside of school and come to see the power of permanently committing their own ideas in writing. They work with children to develop their metalinguistic knowledge, helping them understand the learning strategies that they are being taught and when and why to use a particular form of language.

- employ standard English in their writing, oral reading, questioning, and discussions with their students. They accept and value children's unique modes of expression and distinctive dialects as they guide them toward conventional spelling, speaking, and writing, recognizing that mastery of the conventions of workplace language is the key to future economic success. They, therefore, work with children to help them make choices as to which language to use in which circumstance.

• use dramatic play—spontaneous pretending, dramatization of their own and other people's stories, reenactment of literature— as an important way of supporting reading and writing skills.

• make ample use of print in the classroom environment, providing for children a space rich and stimulating with labels, signs, expressions, and words.

• provide literacy experiences that prepare children for the world of reading, building toward the acquisition of multiple reading strategies, including a variety of text decoding, semantic, and syntactical skills.

• read to children individually and in groups and stimulate thinking about texts by asking questions before, during, and after reading. Children are encouraged to talk about and to write about their ideas and reactions to what they are reading.

• help children learn how to use the library and encourage them to read at home.

• understand the vital interrelationships among speaking, listening, writing, and reading and utilize the children's writing as a process and product to help them develop as readers and conversationalists.

• recognize the importance of social interaction in the development of strong language and literacy skills and provide ongoing opportunities for and facilitate such interaction among children.

• understand the importance of providing children with ample opportunities to select their own reading and writing materials and conversation topics from a rich array of resources so that they may continue to grow and mature as readers and writers.

• understand the complexity involved in developing literacy when the child's first language is not English. They also understand the issues that arise when standard English is not the language a child speaks on a regular basis. They know that language development is tied to culture, and they are careful to take into consideration such factors as the way learning and literacy are valued in the home and the effect that may have on their students. An understanding of the home cultures of their students allows them to adapt their program in ways that increase the prospects for success and maintain high expectations for all children.

Teachers provide varied opportunities for speaking and listening because they understand that both are important to the development of literacy and communication skills. Such activities might include student participation in small groups or whole class discussions, creative dramatics, storytelling, and so on. Teachers use their knowledge of oral language development during these activities to identify children who may benefit from screening and assessment by a specialist.

Early childhood teachers recognize that each of us speaks what is, in effect, a personal dialect reflective of our particular regional upbringing, ethnicity, occupation, age, and socioeconomic class. While teachers celebrate the diversity of language forms in the United States, they also understand that having a shared form of English facilitates communication across societal divisions. Early childhood teachers provide models of "standard" English for the children in their classrooms and encourage students to practice and incorporate its use into their own communication and to know when its use is especially necessary.

Teachers use their knowledge of the typical stages of language and literacy development to assess children's responses. However, they do not simply measure the quantity of children's reading, speaking, listening, and writing as evidence of skill and thoughtfulness. Rather, they employ a process, noticing and recording what children have to say and how children are using language. They then work to build connections between children's present level of knowledge and functioning and more sophisticated levels of performance. Such teachers are also adept at offering suggestions to children about how they can improve their learning and are able to do so without placing a brake on the growth of children's expressive abilities and their desire to continue learning.

MATHEMATICS

Teachers know how children develop concepts and understandings in mathematics, and they use this knowledge in designing and selecting materials and teaching and assessment methods, and in framing discussions and responses to individual children. Their aims are to build children's interest, enjoyment, capability, and curiosity about mathematics. They can explain their teaching strategies in terms of the structure of mathematical concepts, knowledge, procedures, processes, and ideas that define number systems and number sense, geometry, measurement, statistics, probability, and algebra (patterns). They draw on this knowledge and their understanding of the curriculum to plan activities that will deepen children's understanding of and disposition toward mathematics and develop their ability to apply mathematics to everyday problems. Their knowledge of mathematics also helps them select and create a variety of resources, materials, and activities, including manipulative materials, textbooks, newspapers, calculators, computer software, puzzles, and games for counting and studying patterns and charts. Teachers view technology as providing opportunities for children to explore mathematical ideas, to develop concepts, to focus on problem-solving processes, and to investigate realistic applications.

Teachers help children to employ mathematics as a way to explore and solve problems in their environment at home and in school. Their mathematics curriculum capitalizes on children's intuitive insights and language and builds on children's views of themselves as mathematics learners. The children in their classrooms are given many opportunities to construct their own concepts and understandings of numbers and ideas in math through open-ended work with different problems, games, and situations. Children learn to use objects, calculators, computers, charts, graphs, and other materials to help them express ideas and represent problems and solutions in different ways. They exploit opportunities to apply mathematics to everyday situations, for example, helping children to discover the geometric patterns on a leaf during a nature walk. They learn to look for and recognize patterns as a way to form concepts and make sense of problems. For example, teachers use mathematics during field trips, science experiments, literature experiences, cooking and snack times, sports and games, so that students see how they can use mathematics to solve problems, to symbolize phenomena and relationships, and to communicate. Children often work together, exchanging ideas and strategies and learning to appreciate different approaches to problems. Teachers ask questions frequently to clarify how children perceive a problem, develop a strategy, and understand different approaches to reasoning and thinking in mathematics. Children also generate their own questions and propose their own solutions to problems, which they are prepared to explain or defend. Teachers stress understanding concepts rather than an exclusive focus on memorization or speed and accuracy in solving problems. These teachers place the emphasis on increasing children's confidence in their ability to think and communicate mathematically, to solve problems, to make appropriate decisions in selecting strategies and techniques, to recognize familiar structure in unfamiliar settings, and to detect patterns and to analyze data. In part, to accomplish this they integrate mathematics where it naturally fits with subject areas across their curriculum.

SCIENCE

Teachers recognize that young children come to school abounding with natural curiosity about the world and how it works. They know that they can build on children's capabilities in using their senses to acquire information by examining, exploring, comparing, classifying, describing, and asking questions about materials and events in their environment. As children grow, they learn more focused, expanded, and systematic ways to explore their world. Teachers also know that attitudes and dispositions toward science form early. The foundation for equal opportunity for females and members of minority communities to engage science as a means to better understand and enjoy the natural world, as well as to follow career paths in the sciences, must be laid in the early school years. Thus, accomplished teachers seek to support children's enthusiasm, wonder, and curiosity about the world and to increase their understanding of the world.

Teachers are familiar with the big ideas and major concepts of the earth, life, and physical sciences that form the basis of theories and concepts to explain how the world works. They understand the nature of scientific inquiry and the ways in which the scientific community works to test theories and build knowledge over time. They also are familiar with how scientific knowledge is applied in various careers, in inventions and technology, and in addressing a variety of social issues. This knowledge helps them in creating engaging and useful projects and in introducing children to major areas of knowledge and ideas in science. They understand that direct exploration of materials and meaningful phenomena is the cornerstone of science learning for young children. Teachers help children test their own questions and ideas about phenomena and materials in their environment and introduce them to methods of investigation that include predicting, observing, gathering and analyzing data, and inferring and generalizing toward their own hypotheses. They help children pursue multiple paths to investigate a problem, become aware of the scientific nature of their questions, and raise new questions. As a rule, such teachers facilitate children's open exploration of important ideas and concepts, while they simultaneously reinforce children's bringing a scientific frame of mind to their discoveries.

In addition, teachers know that young children typically carry around in their heads roughly formed ideas and a variety of naive misconceptions about how the natural and constructed worlds work. Keeping this in mind, they design experiences that will help children uncover for themselves the counterintuitive nature of many scientific principles and build their knowledge and understanding of science. They recognize that as children have direct experiences with materials and meaningful phenomena, are guided through discrepant experiences, and are solicited to attempt to explain the phenomena they observe, they discover that some of their earlier ideas no longer work. Teachers value the thinking processes that are behind children's naive conceptions and use these as a starting point to design experiences that are likely to help children uncover explanations that may prove to be closer to scientific reality.

Because they know that children learn best by working with concrete materials, employing all their senses, and discussing their ideas, early childhood teachers help children do science rather than only read about it. They design projects, field experiences, and experiments that involve children as investigators and that allow them to build on their own intuitive explanations of how the world works. They set up a rich array of open-ended materials and activities so that children can work with them in a variety of ways guided by their interests and questions. Children are encouraged to talk about their experiences and ideas—to engage their minds rather than simply executing cookbook experiments. Exemplary teachers understand that discussions can transform a class from a collection of individuals to a community of learners sharing their interpretations of the natural world with their peers. Such activities help children to reform and refine their theories and explanations—to learn how to think through their ideas, to pose additional questions, and to reconsider their ideas based on the views of others. Teachers will create extended projects to connect a series of science experiences, often based on unique local circumstances. They provide children with exposure to different tools that they can use to generate and find answers to questions.

Teaching science to young children is closely connected with other aspects of the curriculum, such as using mathematics, deciphering history, and learning about physical health and development and language arts. For example, teachers will often stock the classroom with books and materials about science, read books about science at story time, and offer children this literature during free-choice reading segments of the schedule. Children often work together to generate language experience charts and whole-class journals, individual reports, data sheets and charts, and publication of individual and whole-class books and newspapers about their experiences in learning science.

SOCIAL STUDIES

Teachers know that all children bring to school a wealth of experiences from their families, homes, neighborhoods, and communities. They recognize that, for example, most children have had experiences with siblings or neighbors, most have accompanied parents on errands around town and have had some part in an important family event or celebration. Children with recent immigrant experience in their families have stories and insights that are unique. Teachers use these experiences and the environment of their classrooms or centers to help children begin to understand concepts from the social studies disciplines and to begin to develop the dispositions toward social studies learning that will assure success as their studies progress. They also recognize that children are aware of many of the most visible current events that are featured in the news media or in discussions taking place at home, so they take advantage of this natural background and curiosity and use their knowledge base in economics, government, geography, and history to introduce children to the ways social science looks at issues and events and to begin to introduce their students to the values and cultural norms of other nations and societies. They know that for young children the social studies fundamentally begin with the questioning of who one is and what is his or her place in the world. In addition, there is the natural fascination that young children have with things that are exotic or different from what they know. The diversity within many classrooms provides a starting point for children to begin to understand and value the many distinct cultures of the world. Accomplished teachers take advantage of this opportunity as one of many starting points in their social studies program. They know the importance of children developing the capacity to learn well with others who may come from a different background, and they also know that, for all children, achieving this competency may take time and some assistance from the teacher. They anticipate and know how to respond to children's questions and views about racial, physical, mental, and cultural differences in people they encounter.

In geography, teachers use their grounding in the subject matter to build spatial vocabulary as they orient students to the classroom and the way it changes over time. Literature, art lessons, and field trips are activities that give teachers opportunities to help children learn aspects of physical geography that may not be present in their own immediate environments. As children mature they begin to create their own maps and other representations of their classrooms, homes, and neighborhoods. Teachers also help children understand more formal concepts about the spatial organization of the world and its places and regions and how people interact with the earth.

The area of civics and government allows teachers to help children understand that in their learning communities, just as in their homes, there are rules and rights and responsibilities that allow the classroom to run smoothly. In many classrooms children participate in helping to create and interpret the classroom codes. Students may also be aware of and concerned about problems in their neighborhoods or may be aware of such issues from television. Teachers help young children begin to understand the role that government and its institutions have in addressing problems in their local communities and how these play out through such agencies as the fire and police departments. As children get older, teachers are able to help them understand the broader content of civics and government. They help children learn what government is and the way it works and that, as participants, they can act as agents of change. They work

with children to understand the basic values and principles of American democracy and how constitutional government embodies these purposes, values, and principles. They help children begin to understand the relationship of the United States to other nations in the world and what their roles will be as citizens of this country.

In the area of economics, teachers may use "play" money as a means not only to help children master concepts from mathematics but also to introduce ideas about how the marketplace works. They have knowledge of the fundamental concepts in economics, particularly those that young children can understand. Some classrooms have a store in the play area amply supplied with "money," products, and other props that allow children to assume the roles they have experienced in their communities. Teachers use the scenarios children create as opportunities to extend learning about supply and demand and other concepts from economics. While some ideas from economics are too complex for even the oldest children in this age range, teachers know that children are consumers from an early age and have a keen interest in issues such as scarcity and resource allocation. Teachers find opportunities to incorporate such learning in their curriculum. As an example, they might involve children in a project to determine the amount of food a guinea pig needs each month and then have them figure out how to raise the money for it.

All children come to the classroom with stories to tell, and teachers know that these stories are the groundwork for historical understanding. Teachers are knowledgeable about the major ideas, concepts, and events in United States and world history, as well as the kinds of processes that undergird the historical frame of mind. They use children's own stories as a way to begin the chronological thinking that is critical to historical thinking. A rich array of children's literature provides teachers the opportunity to introduce youngsters to important figures and events from history, as well as to illustrate lessons about character, ethics, and democracy. Sessions designed around the classroom calendar also enhance children's understanding of time, order, and sequence, and national holidays or other special community celebrations or memorials can be a starting point for children's historical learning. In addition to chronological thinking, teachers begin to work with children on historical comprehension, helping them, for example, draw upon data in photographs and other visual images. They start children on the road to historical interpretation, using literature as an opportunity to show the way the same story can be told in several different ways and helping children understand the differences between fact and fiction and the important role of perspective in historical understanding. They help children begin to answer their own historical questions and think analytically, for example, allowing a child to suggest his or her own solution to a problem confronted by a national leader. In addition to assisting the older children in this age group to learn about their own families and communities, teachers help them understand the history of their state, region, and country and how it compares to the history and culture of other nations.

Teachers are skilled at incorporating the ideas from social studies across the curriculum. They know, for example, that understanding the world and its history provides teachers an opportunity to employ legends and mythology from across the globe in their teaching. The goals of history and the social studies—promoting social development, social understanding, democratic ideals, and civic values—lend themselves well to the early learning goals of helping children develop cooperative relationships and mutual respect of their peers. Teachers build the important skills and understandings in these fields in an environment that affords respect to the communities of all their students, and are adept at helping to address the issues that come up as some students have their first experiences with peers and adults who are different from themselves.

STANDARD IV: MULTIPLE TEACHING STRATEGIES FOR MEANINGFUL LEARNING

TEACHERS USE A VARIETY OF METHODS AND MATERIALS TO PROMOTE INDIVIDUAL DEVELOPMENT, MEANINGFUL LEARNING, AND SOCIAL COOPERATION.

Accomplished teachers are diagnosticians and decisionmakers rather than simply implementors of routine methods and activities. They know that young children learn in a variety of ways, so they employ a variety of activities and grouping arrangements and vary their own roles so that students confront important subjects from several angles and through a variety of lenses. This range of techniques allows teachers to create activities that respond to the diversity of their students and to provide each of them with multiple perspectives on key issues, problems, and areas of knowledge, which increase the chances of children coming to grips with important and difficult concepts and ideas.

TEACHERS HAVE A VARIETY OF METHODS TO HELP STUDENTS UNCOVER AND EXPLORE THEIR IDEAS ABOUT WHAT THEY ARE LEARNING

Early childhood teachers use their past experience along with their knowledge of children and subjects to develop an ongoing mix of activities, discussions, and social interactions that allow children to begin to create their own understanding of what they are learning. They model the kind of creative thinking and problem solving that will enable children to become successful in their own endeavors. They are skilled at observing, listening, facilitating discussion, orchestrating play, asking questions, adapting materials and routines to new uses, and helping children make connections with past ideas, experiences, and bodies of knowledge. Teachers ask questions that promote a different focus, that extend or clarify an idea or concept, or that promote deeper or more diverse understandings of the phenomena. In order to add another critical tool to theirs and their students' learning repertoire, teachers help children to develop discussion skills, teaching the importance of listening carefully and responding thoughtfully to the topic at hand. Teachers may present problems or provide explanations as well in the course of an activity or allow students to do so. They may simply provide feedback in the form of a summary or synthesis of what has been said. They encourage children to begin to formulate questions and to develop hypotheses, and they provide and model strategies for organizing and synthesizing information, allowing children to begin to construct their own knowledge and make their own meanings about the world around them. Such teachers intervene as children are working alone or in groups to focus and sustain attention and to provide information or provoke consideration of other questions and angles on an issue that children may seem to have settled. However, they also know when to hold back and let children pursue their own interests and hunches or allow a group to resolve a difficulty or pursue a discussion on its own. Social interaction is a key strategy that teachers employ. Children are encouraged to talk about what they are thinking and experiencing, and teachers understand the importance of such discussions in terms of helping children to reform and refine their theories and explanations—to learn how to think through their ideas, to pose additional questions, and to reconsider their ideas based on the views of others. Teachers call on a battery of effective techniques that encourage learning, including cooperative groups, individualized instruction, and techniques that encourage multiple forms of expression.

TEACHERS MAKE USE OF A VARIETY OF INSTRUCTIONAL MATERIALS

Teachers are knowledgeable about a broad range of instructional resources and adept at selecting, combining, adapting, and creating materials that connect to their larger curricular goals as well as to the experience and interests of their students and that foster learning. They continually seek out and review new books, games, various forms of technology and media, manipulative materials, and experiments as well as find new ways to use familiar items in the classroom. Teachers' choice and design of materials reflect their concerns for child safety as well as the applicability of the materials to different disciplines and learning goals, their potential for multiple forms and levels of engagement, and their connections with student interests and prior experiences. They draw on older students, parents, their peers, and other community members to complement classroom activities. They may also take children to observe and become involved in community events, settings, and institutions.

Teachers recognize the increasing importance of technology as a tool for working with children. They know the ways in which computers can be used to help facilitate the writing process and as a creative medium for a variety of artistic expression. They understand that even preschool children can begin to use basic technological reference sources, such as CD-ROM encyclopedias, to access a variety of information. They are aware of the power of various other technological tools, such as video cameras and synthesizers, to enhance many aspects of their curriculum. Even where such resources are scarce, teachers work to find ways to expose their students to the potential and possibilities they can provide.

TEACHERS CHALLENGE, SUPPORT, AND PROVIDE OPPORTUNITIES FOR STUDENTS TO SUCCEED

Teachers act on the belief that every child can learn, providing high expectations, high support, and engaging, achievable activities for each student on a daily basis. Viewing each child as an individual, teachers assume children will learn and develop at different rates and with different patterns of accomplishment. Teachers understand differences in approaches to learning and patterns of talent, and they design instruction to build on students' strengths as the basis for growth. Therefore, they often select tasks and materials that accommodate a wide range of abilities (e.g., journal writing, creative dramatics, dance, play, computerized instruction, etc.). They are also skilled at strategies that capitalize on different levels of student abilities and interests, such as cooperative learning.

TEACHERS FOSTER STUDENT CAPACITY TO MAKE CHOICES AND WORK AS INDEPENDENT LEARNERS

Accomplished teachers are well organized and purposeful, while pursuing practices that enhance children's autonomy in learning. They help children take responsibility for making appropriate choices about how they spend some of their time each day, how they respond to assignments and experiences, and how they can evaluate their own work. They use a variety of grouping arrangements, including learning centers that allow children to choose activities in different areas of content and development. They provide sufficient time and materials for children to make choices and to pursue questions and interests at some length. They then observe and respond to children's interactions and discourse, taking actions, asking questions, and making suggestions to extend, challenge, and encourage children to elaborate, reflect, or refine their responses.

TEACHERS WORK SUCCESSFULLY WITH CHILDREN WITH EXCEPTIONAL NEEDS

In many classrooms there are children with exceptional needs. Some children's development may fall outside of the range that is typical for their age group; others, for a variety of reasons, may have difficulty with learning; and others may be learning English as a new language. Exemplary teachers recognize such needs and often seek assistance from others to confirm their assessment, to plan services to address these children's needs, and to provide meaningful classroom experiences that are developmentally appropriate. When the child's needs are greater than can be provided for in their own classroom, they support the child and family in seeking alternative settings that better serve the child's needs. They know that families have insights into their children's functioning and adaptation that may not be manifest in the school setting; consequently they make special efforts to learn from those families, to involve them in decisionmaking, and to inform them of the child's progress. They also work cooperatively with a variety of specialists, such as speech/language pathologists, English-language development or bilingual educators, physical and occupational therapists, special educators, psychologists, and other specialists in child development.

With these specialists, teachers plan, adapt, and implement classroom practices and activities that are individually appropriate while simultaneously ensuring that each child becomes an important and valued member of the class. They create an environment to help children learn about each other and understand that each individual has capacities and limitations that make him or her unique. Teachers take care to adapt their practice to accommodate these children and, when necessary, seek appropriate support services to ensure their success. They also respond to children who need to concentrate on a narrower set of outcomes, who would benefit from a more systematic approach to refining skills, or who bring unusual gifts or talents to the classroom, and they do so without compromising their commitment to promoting thinking, conceptual development, problem solving, and social relationships.

STANDARD V: ASSESSMENT

TEACHERS KNOW THE STRENGTHS AND WEAKNESSES OF VARIOUS ASSESSMENT METHODOLOGIES, CONTINUALLY MONITOR CHILDREN'S ACTIVITIES AND BEHAVIOR, AND ANALYZE THIS INFORMATION TO IMPROVE THEIR WORK WITH CHILDREN AND PARENTS.

Accomplished early childhood teachers are regular and insightful observers of young children at work and at play. Assessment is not a separate event in the classroom calendar but rather a daily, ongoing activity. Given the importance of understanding the developmental levels of children, teachers examine a variety of forms of evidence of growth, stability, and patterns in how children speak, interact with peers, and carry out learning tasks. Such teachers are skilled in identifying and responding to classroom concerns, recognizing problems in social relationships, identifying opportunities for a new level of learning, or perceiving unusual stress or excitement in children. As well as these informal methods of assessment, teachers create more formal systems to identify children's knowledge and emerging capacities. They use assessment for a variety of purposes, the first of which is to help themselves judge the effects of their work and to inform their own practice. In addition, they use their observations to help children and parents understand and celebrate progress. Teachers are also committed to being accountable to the public for their practice, working with colleagues to promote public understanding of the aims and achievements of the schools.

TEACHERS USE A VARIETY OF APPROACHES FOR ASSESSING CHILDREN

Teachers assess all the goals of their practice, collecting and analyzing information on how children are growing cognitively, socially, physically, and emotionally. In assessing learning, teachers' concerns are not confined to children's level of factual knowledge. Rather, teachers also record and analyze

- the forms of children's responses;
- the processes children employ in creating products, solving problems, and arriving at answers; and
- children's patterns of persistence and curiosity and their ability to work with peers and adults and a variety of materials.

Accordingly, teachers use a mix of assessment strategies and assess children over time in different settings, employing

- ongoing observations, questioning, and listening to get at what and how children are thinking;
- systematic procedures to create anecdotal records of how children spend their time, their social relationships, the modes of learning that seem particularly engaging to or productive for them and their use of language;
- systematic sampling of children's activities and performance, including collecting examples of their writing, artwork, audiotapes of oral reading, dictated stories, literature response logs, and records of group participation in projects; and
- standardized instruments when they are appropriate, accurate, and an efficient part of a multistage assessment or diagnostic process.

Teachers process assessment data against several frames of reference:

- the unfolding picture of the individual child as a learner and person, which sets a context for judging changes in skills, knowledge, concepts, dispositions, and behaviors;

- a map of typical stages and patterns of learning in young children; and
- a collective portrait of the classroom, which provides insights in interpreting the information they collect.

Teachers encourage children to develop skills at judging their own work and the work of their peers and others. For example, they ask children to express opinions and to notice patterns of similarities and differences in stories and poetry; to contribute and receive comments on drafts of a story or report; to choose and explain their preferences for particular pieces of work over a period of time; and to listen critically in discussions and oral presentations.

TEACHERS USE ASSESSMENT TO INFORM THEIR INSTRUCTION

Teachers are skilled in noticing children whose growth and development are somehow unusual or outside the normal range that might be expected. They can distinguish between children who should be referred for screening and assessment to identify possible disabilities and those whose learning and behavioral problems are likely to be temporary or indicative of a need to change classroom routines, activities, or social supports. If need be, they are effective team members in such assessment and planning procedures, contributing specific observations and insights from the child's classroom learning and behavior. They understand the major types of disabilities and

the general state-of-the-art of assessment technology. They also know how to involve parents in the assessment process, in developing Individual Education Programs or Individual Family Service Programs, and in monitoring and revising these plans. They take responsibility for communicating with other staff who work with their students and with their students' next year's teachers, conveying insights on their abilities, interests, and receptivity to different instructional strategies.

Early childhood teachers are well informed about current research on assessment in the early childhood years. They are cognizant of controversies regarding testing, the problems of inappropriate use of test data (e.g., when such data are used as the sole determinant to retain young children in their current grade), as well as positive trends in the development of more comprehensive, meaningful, and constructive forms of observational and performance-based forms of assessment for young children.

Teachers may have to deal with situations in which a program, school district, or state mandates tests that are flawed or that fail to reflect the full range of goals in learning and development. In such situations highly accomplished teachers do not allow these practices to exert a detrimental influence on their work with children. In addition, they work to advocate changes in assessment policy so that testing practices are aligned with effective instructional practices. They also communicate effectively with parents to explain the significance and limits of test data.

Standard VI: Reflective Practice

Teachers regularly analyze, evaluate, and strenghten the quality and effectiveness of their work.

Accomplished teachers consider reflection on their practice central to their responsibilities as professionals to steadily extend their knowledge, perfect their teaching, and refine their evolving philosophy of education. They examine their strengths and needed area of improvement and employ that knowledge in their analysis and planning. They understand that the impact of specific lessons, textbooks, strategies, assignments, or assessment tools may vary from class to class as the mix of children changes. They analyze the needs of their students in relation to both the circumstances of the moment and their long-term objectives. They evaluate the relative merits of teaching practices considered exemplary and judge their appropriateness for their own particular circumstances. Consequently, such teachers distinguish themselves by their capacity for ongoing, dispassionate self-examination, their openness to innovation, and their willingness to change in order to strengthen their teaching.

While there are no cookbook guides to accomplished practice, new information about teaching, the subjects under consideration, and child development proliferates. Thus, teachers who stand still are, in fact, moving rapidly backward. Motivated both by the change they see around them and by the desire to equip students for a changing future, they regularly engage in the process of professional growth. Two valuable sources of such growth are self-reflection aided by interaction with other professionals and self-renewal through exploration of new resources, the study of professional literature, and participation in advanced education programs.

Teachers Evaluate Results and Seek Input Systematically from a Variety of Sources

For accomplished teachers every class and every activity provides opportunities for reflection and improvement. When things go well, they think about why the class succeeded and how to adapt the lessons learned to other classes. When things go poorly, they reflect on how to avoid such mishaps in the future. When they review the work-in-progress and final products of their students, these teachers assess themselves as well as their students. Their conversations with children about classroom climate and interactions provide them with insight and direction. They also carefully analyze input received from parent-child-teacher conferences, parent-teacher conferences, and informal conversations with family members. On a regular basis these teachers seek knowledge and advice from colleagues through discussions, in-class observation of their own teaching, and personal observation of other teachers' practice. These observations and discussions shape their decisions about if, when, and how their practice should change and create a predisposition to abandon less-effective practices and replace them with more-promising approaches.

Teachers Are Open to New Ideas and Continually Refine Their Practice

Given the dynamics at work in the profession, the introspection of exemplary teachers ranges from consideration of the role that their own cultural background, biases, values, and personal experiences play in their teaching through participation in seminars, workshops, and courses that challenge their current thinking. They may conduct action research in their classrooms or collaborate with educational researchers to examine their practice critically. They are models of the educated individual as they sharpen their judgment, expand their repertoire of teaching methods, and deepen their knowledge base. This includes keeping abreast of significant developments and debates in the disciplines. Such efforts are essential, for research in early learning is ongoing and dynamic, and ideas about practice change regularly. Concurrently, the profession is steadily rethinking, reinventing, and debating a broad range of pedagogical and content issues that have curricular implications.

These teachers consider the prevailing research findings about young children, learning, and intelligence while being aware of their limitations. They are able to distinguish fads from real breakthroughs, fashions from knowledge—conscious that not all ideas about how practice should change are good ones. They stay current with and evaluate professional and other literature and curricular materials and also the issues affecting families and schooling in their community. They take

responsibility for their own professional growth, which might include keeping a personal journal, having regular discussions with colleagues, or taking coursework at local universities. They select from theories, emerging practices, current debates, and promising research findings those that could improve their practice. In doing so, they explore topics in which they may have limited expertise and experiment with alternative materials, approaches, and instructional strategies. They also draw on formal and informal findings from their own practice as an ongoing guide to setting the future direction of their work. This personal study provides support for the instructional decisions they make and for their ability to articulate cogently a rationale for their actions. It also contributes to their consistent ability to be aggressive in seeking solutions to issues and problems in their practice.

Exemplary teachers participate in a wide range of reflective practices that reinforce their creativity, stimulate their personal growth, and enhance their professionalism. They exemplify the highest ethical ideals and embrace professional standards in assessing their practice. Ultimately, self-reflection contributes to teachers' depth of knowledge, skills, and dispositions and adds dignity to their practice.

Standard VII: Family Partnerships

Teachers work with and through parents and families to support children's learning and development.

The engagement of parents and guardians in their children's education is of inestimable value to the accomplished early childhood teacher. These teachers view their students' families as allies in their work, recognize the dependence of young children on their families, know that parental affirmation of the school staff and program is important to children's motivation and sense of well-being in the classroom, and understand that the school's affirmation of the child's home culture is important to the child's well-being and to the ability of the home to support the child and the school.

Teachers are respectful of the varying types of families they work with, understanding that their patterns of child rearing and values and beliefs about education may differ from the teacher's own. Teachers gauge each parent's special abilities, interests, and "comfort zone" regarding involvement in their child's education. They then respond with a range of options to encourage parent involvement, such as observing in the classroom, working as a regular volunteer, or assisting in the creation of materials at home.

Early childhood teachers recognize the complexities and tensions common in working with families. Communicating with and involving parents is complex even when families and professionals speak the same language and share opinions and values. It is clearly more difficult when they disagree. Teachers recognize the need for consultation and negotiation about differences in values, relationships, and routines. They do not presume that the school culture is superior to the home environment and values, and they ex-hibit a problem-solving orientation over time in their work with parents.

Teachers Communicate Effectively with Parents and Families to Inform and Enhance Support for Children's Learning

Teachers are skilled in listening, observing, and learning from family members. They are also adept in conveying information and ideas to parents so that parents understand how their child is doing, what the teacher is doing and seeking to accomplish, and what families can do to complement, enrich, and extend school-based learning.

Teachers are eager to listen to and learn from parents, because parents are especially knowledgeable about the past development and present attributes of their children. They solicit parents' goals and priorities for their child, reports of children's responses to program experiences and relationships, and information on how the child functions at home and in the community. They use a variety of means to learn from families, which may include home visits and simple written surveys. They listen actively and patiently to make sure they understand what parents have to say. They make special efforts to seek out parents who are less aggressive or open in expressing their views. Teachers are also careful to respect the confidentiality of information provided by parents, while using it to cross-check their own perceptions of how children are doing.

Early childhood teachers provide parents with information about their programs and children's progress in school. They explain the rationale for their major goals, activities, and teaching methods. They offer opportunities for conferences and meetings at the convenience of parents and seek to provide information in a language that parents should be able to understand. Teachers are honest in communicating with families, telling them what goes on in the classroom and admitting when they are not sure about how to resolve an issue or problem. They place a priority on regular communication with parents about each child's progress. They use a number of methods to explain assessment procedures and results, including written reports, regular samples of children's work with teacher comments, and formal conferences. Last, but not least, they find occasions to celebrate with parents their children's accomplishments.

TEACHERS WORK EFFECTIVELY WITH FAMILY AND COMMUNITY VOLUNTEERS IN CLASSROOM AND SCHOOL ACTIVITIES

Teachers are comfortable in working with and coordinating the efforts of a variety of people to help them meet their objectives. They understand how the presence of family and community members provides support to individual children and to the different cultural groups that may be represented in the classroom. Consequently, parents are always welcome to visit the classroom. Teachers actively solicit family members to serve as volunteers (including fathers and male family members, grandparents and senior citizens from the community, and older students) and offer a variety of options for involvement (e.g., preparing materials for projects, presenting experiences to the class or a small group, supporting a particular child with an immediate need). They recognize that not all who assist in their classrooms come well prepared with the skills necessary to work productively

with young children. They, therefore, actively supervise and provide guidance and support to the parents, volunteers, and aides who work alongside them to enhance the learning environment. They anticipate and head off problems (such as volunteers gossiping about classroom events or using inappropriate language or disciplinary procedures) by orienting and debriefing volunteers and observers and providing clear explanations about classroom norms and routines.

TEACHERS ASSIST FAMILIES IN SUPPORTING CHILDREN'S LEARNING AND DEVELOPMENT AT HOME

Teachers share information about child development and learning that parents can apply at home. They are knowledgeable about programs and materials for parent education and support, and they provide resources that parents can use to extend and complement classroom learning activities. They encourage and assist parents in sharpening their ability to observe and understand their child's behavior and discourse. They respond to parents' questions and observations about children's growth, development, behavior, and language at home.

TEACHERS WORK EFFECTIVELY WITH PARENTS IN DECISIONMAKING ROLES AND ON POLICY ISSUES

Early childhood teachers acknowledge parents as citizens, taxpayers, and crucial clients of schools and early childhood programs. They explain the rationale for major changes in areas such as curriculum, materials, testing, or special programs and seek parental input before implementing such changes. They work effectively with parent representatives in planning or reviewing school programs. They invite participation from all types of parents in committees and advisory groups. They are also skilled in participating with parents in special education service planning and assessments, and they are cognizant of parents' due-process rights in these settings.

TEACHERS ASSIST FAMILIES IN OBTAINING SUPPORTS AND SERVICES TO HELP THEIR CHILDREN

Teachers exercise good judgment in working to help meet the needs of families and children. They understand their capabilities and limitations in responding to stresses and problems in the lives of families. They recognize the value at times of simply listening with empathy to parents' concerns as well as the value in other situations when referring parents to other people in the school system or other agencies is the most appropriate course of action. They also can assist families in engaging peers and networks for information and social support.

Teachers know about the amalgam of related services for families and children that are often available from the school system, agencies, and informal neighborhood organizations. They are alert to evidence of needs in children and families in areas such as health examinations and services, social and recreational opportunities, adult literacy and employment training, respite care and mental health services, income support or employment opportunities, and services to children or adults with disabilities. In particular, preschool teachers are familiar with kindergarten and primary-grade programs and help families in preparing to participate successfully in their child's elementary school. Similarly, exemplary kindergarten and primary-grade teachers have working relationships with other early childhood programs in the community. They know about the experiences children have had prior to entering elementary school, and they can assist families in seeking support from other early childhood agencies.

Standard VIII: Professional Partnerships

TEACHERS WORK WITH COLLEAGUES TO IMPROVE PROGRAMS AND PRACTICES FOR YOUNG CHILDREN AND THEIR FAMILIES.

Accomplished teachers are able to work effectively with supervisors, aides, peers, professionals from other disciplines, and volunteers. They work to overcome structures or traditions that separate teachers from each other and seek to make the school a collaborative enterprise that draws out the best from its faculty. And they work to build and strengthen a community of professional educators committed to the healthy development of young children.

Teachers Are Skilled at Working with a Variety of Other People in Providing Effective Early Childhood Education

Teachers know how to give and receive support, advice, feedback, and criticism from each other. They know what is involved in training and coordinating the variety of adults who often fall under their supervision in early childhood programs. They work to develop regular forums for talking with peers about how to improve their collective efforts. They are skilled in identifying and celebrating successes as well as reconciling conflicts with colleagues, parents, and administrators. They are able to challenge other people whose behavior is detrimental to children or other adults. They also contribute effectively to assessment teams and processes with other professionals from health, mental health, special education, and social work. They can contribute their observations and insights on the classroom and draw implications from the in-

sights of staff from other disciplines. In order to better articulate the school program, they consult with teachers in earlier and later grades for background as to how the children have been prepared and to understand how well they are preparing students to move ahead.

Teachers Contribute to the Professional Development of Colleagues and Support Staff

In many early childhood programs with differentiated and multiple staff roles, early childhood teachers are responsible for planning and supervising the work of an instructional team while also continuing to work directly with children. Such teachers are effective in training, managing, and monitoring less-experienced staff members (see "Standard VII—Family Partnerships"). They are capable of assessing the knowledge, abilities, and strengths of team members, creating appropriate assignments, encouraging and contributing to their professional growth, and providing appropriate feedback and support as they work with children.

Teachers show skill in communicating their knowledge of child development and early childhood teaching principles to aides, assistant teachers, and volunteers in the context of everyday work. They use a variety of techniques and resources to promote the development of other staff, such as reading, discussing, modeling, observing, and providing feedback; work jointly to develop materials or carry out an activity; and do group planning as well as the more formal evaluation and training activities provided through the school program.

TEACHERS UNDERSTAND AND PARTICIPATE IN SHAPING POLICIES THAT INFLUENCE THEIR WORK WITH CHILDREN

Early childhood teachers face special challenges in their work due to the vulnerability of young children and the variety of programs and institutions that provide early childhood education. They understand how policies have a major impact on their work and the children they teach, including such areas as

- curriculum, testing, grouping, and promotion standards;
- time for planning, developing materials, and analyzing assessment information on children;
- adult-to-child ratios and class size;
- physical space, equipment, and materials; and
- the conduct of teacher evaluations.

Teachers seek an active role in and can productively contribute to the formulation of such policies. Because early childhood teachers work in a wide variety of contexts (ranging from highly favorable and supportive environments to settings with many barriers), there is no single ideal stance for teachers to assume in responding to policy influences. However, in all cases they work to educate policymakers, parents, and citizens on the underlying principles of excellence in early childhood education and to help them understand how these principles might be best translated into programmatic initiatives within their own particular context. They also understand the basic structure and sources of policy that influence the setting where they work with children, including mechanisms such as licensing standards for child care centers, the

Head Start performance standards and monitoring system, and major federal education programs, such as Title I and legislation governing services to young children with disabilities. They seek to shape attitudes and opinions by taking the initiative in suggesting to other educators and to the lay community those readings, conferences, and opportunities to observe classrooms and programs that will inform their thinking regarding early childhood education.

When they are given the opportunity, exemplary teachers are effective participants in decision making. They use their knowledge of the children and the community, their understanding of educational research, and their abilities to work with peers to fashion creative approaches to issues, such as curriculum, assessment, and allocating material resources and staff. When they are faced with educationally inappropriate mandates, they can articulate their concerns to administrators and policymakers and devise creative responses that safeguard the interests of children.

TEACHERS CONTRIBUTE TO EARLY CHILDHOOD EDUCATION

Through giving workshops, networking, participating in professional organizations, writing, and other such means, teachers are involved with the advancement of early childhood education. Some choose to become involved in issues or service in their local communities that have an impact on the children they are serving. They may also contribute to new knowledge through action research in their classrooms, collaborative projects with researchers, presentations, and more informal reflection and sharing of ideas and practices with colleagues.

EPILOGUE

These eight standards provide a profile of the accomplished Early Childhood/ Generalist teacher. While, in sum, they may seem extraordinarily demanding, every day they are upheld by teachers like the ones who live in these pages, who are hard at work in our schools inspiring the nation's children. Too many teachers go unnoticed and unappreciated. National Board Certification holds the potential to change this state of affairs.

These standards also promise to be a stimulus for self-reflection on the part of teachers at all levels of performance and a catalyst for a healthy debate and the forging of a new professional consensus on exemplary practice in this field. If these standards can advance the conversation about excellence in teaching in these directions, they will provide an important step toward satisfying the National Board's aims to improve student learning in America's schools.

Early Childhood/Generalist
Standards Committee

Baiba Woodall—*Chair*
First Grade Teacher
Trumansburg Central School
Trumansburg, New York

Mary Zapata Huerta—*Vice Chair*
Kindergarten Teacher
Woodlawn Elementary School
San Antonio, Texas

Leslee Bartlett
Second/Third Grade Teacher
Washington School
Salt Lake City, Utah

Barbara T. Bowman
President
Erikson Institute for
    Child Development
Chicago, Illinois

Barbara J. Bushey
Kindergarten Teacher
Conant School
Bloomfield Hills, Michigan

Margaret Eriacho
Second Grade Teacher
A:Shiwi Elementary School
Zuni, New Mexico

Barbara M. Flores
Associate Professor of
    Elementary and Bilingual Education
California State University/San Bernardino
San Bernardino, California

Donna B. Foglia
Assistant Principal
Norwood Creek School
Evergreen School District
San Jose, California

Joyce Jech
Principal
Marrs Elementary School
Skiatook, Oklahoma

John M. Johnston
Professor
Early Childhood Teacher Education
University of Memphis
Memphis, Tennessee

Sharon Lynn Kagan
Senior Associate
The Bush Center in Child
    Development and Social Policy
Yale University
New Haven, Connecticut

Juanita M. Robinson
Head Start Teacher
Bells Mill Elementary School
Potomac, Maryland

Yvonne Smith
Prekindergarten Teacher
Central Park East School
New York, New York

Mark R. Wolery
Senior Research Scientist
Child and Family Studies Program
Allegheny-Singer Research Institute
Pittsburgh, Pennsylvania

Acknowledgments

The Early Childhood/Generalist standards are among the first sets of standards to be developed by the National Board for Professional Teaching Standards (NBPTS) for the advanced certification of teachers. As such, they are the product of invention by many people who worked with the Early Childhood/Generalist Standards Committee to craft them, including the NBPTS Board of Directors and its Certification Standards Working Group, which provided the process with careful guidance, loving criticism, and much encouragement. The National Board, with the able assistance of this committee, sought not only to forge a professional consensus about the critical aspects of highly accomplished practice in this field but also to develop a model for constructing advanced teaching standards that would speak clearly and powerfully to prospective candidates for National Board Certification, to the early childhood community, to the larger education community, and to the public.

Many individuals and institutions contributed to this effort. Teachers, scholars, administrators, state and local officials, education association leaders, and others from across the country critically reviewed draft standards, provided sound advice about how to strengthen the standards, and helped position the standards so that they might complement other initiatives designed to advance practice in this field. While a variety of people unstintingly provided the National Board with caring, intelligent, and imaginative counsel, several deserve special thanks. The members of the Early Childhood/Generalist Standards Committee, a group of exceptionally dedicated, creative, and industrious professionals, did the heavy lifting that yielded this new vision of accomplished practice. They were ably led by Baiba Woodall and Mary Zapata Huerta, who kept the teacher's perspective in the forefront and helped forge a consensus around large principles when lesser solutions were also available. Nettie Webb, the Board's liaison to the committee, made important contributions to advancing and uplifting the debate across a range of critical issues. Yolanda Rodriguez worked tirelessly and creatively to organize and facilitate the debate early in the life of the committee and was ably assisted by Tom Schultz, who employed his sharp pen and good ear to craft the initial draft standards. David Haynes served as the lead staff and principal scribe during the latter part of this project, uncovering difficult issues and developing solutions when the committee reached an impasse and providing elegant prose to capture the committee's distinct perspective. The committee's final deliberations also were enlightened by the work of the Assessment Development Laboratory established at the Educational Development Center, led by Joanne Brady. Last, but not least, this initiative benefited from the good counsel of Sue Bredekamp of the National Association for the Education of Young Children and Laura Roehler of the International Reading Association and their colleagues in each organization, who provided constructive critiques when the draft standards were circulated for review.

In the end, the National Board for Professional Teaching Standards takes full responsibility for these standards, but the standards would not have received as positive a reception as they have without the wisdom, intelligence, and care of those who have willingly given of their time and energy to this landmark effort to improve American education.

INFORMATION ABOUT NAEYC

NAEYC is . . .

. . . a membership-supported organization of people committed to fostering the growth and development of children from birth through age 8. Membership is open to all who share a desire to serve and act on behalf of the needs and rights of young children.

NAEYC provides . . .

. . . educational services and resources to adults who work with and for children, including

- *Young Children, the* journal for early childhood educators
- **books, posters, brochures,** and **videos** to expand your knowledge and commitment to young children, with topics including infants, curriculum, research, discipline, teacher education, and parent involvement
- an **Annual Conference** that brings people together from all over the country to share their expertise and advocate on behalf of children and families
- **Week of the Young Child** celebrations sponsored by NAEYC Affiliate Groups across the nation to call public attention to the needs and rights of children and families
- **insurance plans** for individuals and programs
- **public affairs** information and access to information available through NAEYC resources and communication systems for knowledgeable advocacy efforts at all levels of government and through the media
- the **National Academy of Early Childhood Programs,** a voluntary accreditation system for high-quality programs for children
- the **National Institute for Early Childhood Professional Development,** which offers resources and services to improve professional preparation and development of early childhood educators
- **Young Children International** to promote international communication and information exchanges

For free information about membership, publications, or other NAEYC services, contact

National Association for the Education
   of Young Children
1509 16th Street, NW
Washington, DC 20036-1426
202-232-8777 or 1-800-424-2460